A Summer
That Can Change
Your Life:

*A History of the
Educational Opportunity Program
at Central Connecticut State University*

C. J. JONES
TOM HAZUKA

woodhall press

NORWALK, CONNECTICUT

Library of Congress Cataloging-in-Publication Data available
978-1-949116-04-5

Woodhall Press
81 Old Saugatuck Road, Norwalk, CT 06855
WoodhallPress.com

Distributed by INGRAM

This book is dedicated to all Educational Opportunity Program students and staff, and to the many individuals directly and indirectly associated with EOP. You have enriched our lives and brought us a lifetime of memories. The effects of EOP on generations are amazing, far beyond anything we could have imagined. EOP is truly "a summer that has changed lives," including ours.

Linda & C. J. Jones

"Education then, beyond other devices of human origin, is a great equalizer of the conditions of men—the balance-wheel of the social machinery."

—*Horace Mann*

Contents

The EOP Creed

So, then, to all persons their chance—
To all persons, regardless of their birth,
Their shining, golden opportunity—
To all persons the right to live,
To work, to be themselves,
And to become
Whatever things their humanity and their vision
Can combine to make them—
This, seekers,
Is the promise of America.

—A paraphrasing of the words of Thomas Wolfe

Introduction

This book is both a celebration and an exploration. I knew about the celebration part before writing a word: the fiftieth anniversary of Central Connecticut State University's Educational Opportunity Program in 2018. As someone involved with the EOP almost from the beginning, and its director for twenty-five years, I've had this golden anniversary marked on my mental calendar for some time now. The EOP has played a major role in hundreds of lives, not least my own, and a party is definitely in order.

That said, my impressions of the EOP's impact have been mostly anecdotal. I've kept in touch with quite a few EOP "kids" (sorry, it's hard for me to think of them any other way) after graduation, following their successful lives—and their children's lives, and in some cases their grandchildren's. Others I've heard about second- and third-hand. But there hasn't been a systematic study of the EOP's effects. Obviously, I think those effects are positive and worthwhile, or I wouldn't have directed the program for over two decades. But believing something and having empirical proof are two different animals.

As of the 2017–2018 academic year, more than 2,000 students have participated in the Central Connecticut State University EOP. Many thousands more have been part of similar programs at other Connecticut colleges, including Southern and Eastern

Connecticut State Universities, and Wesleyan University, and in states such as California, New York and Texas. How useful has EOP been to their lives, and by extension, how useful to American society? Most EOP participants have come from minority populations as first-generation college students. In the early days of the program (and possibly still today) some people attached a certain stigma to those categories, and therefore to the EOP's mission. Were these suspicions justified, or have the EOP's results put the lie to them? Is this sort of program a feel-good waste of money, or can it create lasting, generational change that pays for itself many times over?

My answers to those questions are no secret. Now let's take a look at the evidence.

"The Golden Opportunity"

Central Connecticut State University[1] mathematics professor George Wyer hatched the idea for CCSU's Educational Opportunity Program in 1968. In George's words, "I was teaching Mathematics courses for prospective K-12 teachers. Observing a fair number of minority background students who seemed quite talented yet a step or two behind in Mathematics, English and study skills, I set down some criteria (assumptions) for overcoming such limiting factors. Thus was born the Educational Opportunity Program, which I directed and taught the Mathematics in for the first two summers. The design validated, I turned the EOP over to Charles (C. J.) Jones." Wyer's thesis was simple but profound in its implications: Give six weeks of summer instruction to disadvantaged but motivated students who do not yet qualify for admission to Central, then create an ongoing support structure for them, and most will succeed in college.

Possibly as a sign of the times, the CCSU administration was open to the idea. 1968 was a turbulent year in the United States

---

1. The school was actually Central Connecticut State College until becoming a university in 1983, but for simplicity's sake I'll refer to it throughout as Central Connecticut State University.

(though on the positive side, my Detroit Tigers won the World Series). Colleges, including CCSU, were no exception to the controversy. There were widespread campus protests against the Vietnam War. Martin Luther King Jr. and Robert Kennedy were assassinated. At the Mexico City Olympics, Tommie Smith and John Carlos gave black power salutes on the medal stand, just one indication of the simmering racial tension in American society. The Black Panthers, and Angela Davis's political feminism, were constantly in the national news. In 1968 CCSU wasn't an all-white institution, but it was pretty close. There were more black students than when I arrived in 1964, but not a lot more, and most of them were athletes like me. I'm sure the administration wanted to increase minority enrollment, because it was the right thing to do, because "the times they were a-changing," and because failure to be more inclusive would lead to bad press. Whatever the motivations, Wyer's EOP proposal was approved on a trial basis by Central's faculty and administration. That is, the program was given initial funding, with ongoing support dependent on how well it succeeded in its mission.

The first EOP class met in the summer of 1969, with thirty-one students. Everything was new, so there was definitely some trial and error involved, but all of the students completed the program. The success of that first group convinced the administration that the EOP experiment deserved continued support and led to bigger EOP classes (eventually with around fifty students) in subsequent years. (In 2017 that number rose to sixty-four students; more on that later.) Funding was also provided to hire additional staff, and to extend EOP activities beyond the summer to the regular academic year—a vital improvement to ensure that lessons learned during the summer were reinforced and built upon. It also offered crucial support to students from families with no experience of higher education, who could therefore not count on much help from home with the transition to college life and college-level work.

I graduated from CCSU in 1969 and am the first to admit that I would have greatly benefited if EOP had existed when I was a freshman. I was a decent student at Bayside High School in Queens, New York, but had few educational role models. No one in my family had gone to college, much less earned a degree. My family wasn't anti-education by any means; college simply wasn't part of our universe. It's a matter of expectations. If you grow up playing golf and tennis at a country club, chances are you'll belong to a country club when you're older. Of course you'll go to college, and probably a prestigious one. It's a given; it's what people like your family and friends do. Making a new path for yourself, without the benefit of well-marked family and social group highways, is a heck of a lot harder. In fact, without some help it's almost impossible.

I think my personal story is a good example of how no one succeeds totally on their own. My journey to Central Connecticut State University began long before I realized I'd set foot on that path. I grew up in the Bronx, New York, but by my early teens my parents had separated and my mother was working full-time as a court clerk to support us. Our neighborhood wasn't the greatest, and my mother wanted a more stable environment and a better school system for me. My older sister and her husband had moved to Bayside, Queens, so I went to live with them, and attended Marie Curie Junior High and Bayside High School. Most weekends I'd take the bus to the Bronx to visit my mother. How would my life have turned out if I had stayed in the Bronx? I'll never know, but I truly doubt it would have been better.

I'll also never know how my life would have turned out if I hadn't been smitten by the dream of playing college basketball—which was also influenced by my being in Queens. The 1964 US Olympic basketball tryouts took place at St. John's University, just a few blocks from Bayside High School, so I could easily attend the sessions. Watching players like Bill Bradley, Walt Hazzard, Bad News Barnes, Jeff Mullins, and Larry Brown—yes, the one who became a famous coach in college and the National Basketball Association —I knew that no matter what else I did in life, I wanted to play college basketball.

Fortunately for me, I got help—and got lucky. Often the cliché is true that it's not what you know, it's who you know. People like me didn't have a lot of contacts, a lot of "ins," but you only need one if it's the right one. My high school counselor was John Nucatola, a future Hall of Fame referee and head of officials for the NBA. He happened to referee a CCSU game, and after a conversation with Central coach Bill Detrick thought I might be a good fit for CCSU's program. My college choices came down to American University in Washington, DC, and CCSU. It became a strictly financial decision, where a partial scholarship at American would cost significantly more than CCSU. So CCSU it was.

I got to live out my dream of playing college basketball. I was no big star, but I participated in a National Collegiate Athletic Association (NCAA) tournament (CCSU was Division II at the time), took my first-ever plane flight (to Akron, Ohio), and thoroughly enjoyed being on the team. One of my personal highlights was being fouled late in a game at Albany and hitting two free throws for the win. Truth be told, my main impact on basketball at Central Connecticut would come later, first as an assistant coach, then interim head coach, and finally as athletics director, when I would hire former teammate Howie Dickenman, a legendary figure in the state, as head coach. Dickenman led our team to its first winning season in Division I, three NCAA tournament appearances, and a string of sixteen consecutive conference tournament appearances.

I had planned to be a high school physical education teacher, and I received job offers at two Hartford high schools: Hartford Public (where I had student taught) and Weaver. But I finished at CCSU in December and did not want to start a job in the middle of the school year. I knew how challenging teaching in the inner city would be, let alone starting halfway through the year, so I decided a fresh start would be better. I began working on my master's degree at Central while working in the registrar's office.

In the summer of 1970, an opportunity came up to join George Wyer as codirector of the EOP. This was the second time my whole life changed because of who I knew, and because I was in the right place at the right time. My guidance counselor John Nucatola put me on the path that led to CCSU, and CCSU registrar Carl Beck led me to a job I loved and would hold for the next twenty-five years. Carl must have liked the work I was doing as a graduate assistant in his office, and he recommended me for the EOP codirector position.

There was actually another interesting factor in the situation. The previous fall, on October 21, 1969, a group of twenty or so black students had taken over the CCSU administration building. Takeovers of university administration buildings by student activists were not uncommon during this era, often to protest the Vietnam War. The CCSU protest, however, concerned race relations at the school and how to improve them. The students presented a list of twenty demands to the administration, including:

> More white students be brought before university officials and suspended for incidents that occurred on campus (bottles were thrown at black students)
>
> An increase in minority population to 15 percent, closer to the population of Connecticut, rather than the current 6–8 percent at CCSU
>
> Twenty more black faculty members (there were only two, both in Art, Al Martin and Betty King)
>
> An Afro-American Studies major
>
> Black members on the board of trustees
>
> *A revised Educational Opportunity Program because the present director was not sufficient or relevant to the black student body.*

Obviously, the last demand is the one that most concerns this book. This is a complex issue for me. I was not part of the group that took over the administration building. I was not asked to join the protest, and in fact had no idea it would be happening. Although I have no firm proof of this, I strongly suspect that my interracial relationship with fellow CCSU student Linda Coggshall was one reason for not trying to include me. (Linda and I got married in 1974 and are together to this day.) In addition, I socialized to a large degree with my teammates, and most of them were white. If I *had* been asked I almost surely would have declined. I was busy student teaching at Hartford Public

High School and set to graduate in December, and I wanted to stay on that course.

So when I joined EOP in 1970, it wasn't necessarily a popular decision among the African-American community at CCSU. I filled the demand for a black EOP director, but for some people I wasn't "black enough." To be honest I couldn't have cared less. I was confident that my experience would make me relevant to EOP participants, and that was all that mattered.

Until I joined the program, I had only a faint inkling of what EOP was about. I'd heard of it but didn't know many details. I learned quickly, though, interacting with George Wyer and the kids. I also learned a lot about myself that summer. George and I had contrasting personalities. He was an analytical math professor, pretty straitlaced and not very flexible. I had graduated with a degree in English and was more of a liberal arts-type of person. Our time together taught me valuable lessons about compromising and working with people.

I lived in a dorm with the students. With my background, I understood their issues and their struggles. I let George take the lead while I acted as a sounding board for the kids and staff. I had to walk a fine line, making sure not to undermine George's authority while I reassured participants that everything was being done in their best interests, and though they might not understand now, they would in the future.

Speaking of the future, after that summer George decided the additional EOP responsibilities were too taxing on him and his family, so he left EOP and returned to just teaching. The students' demand for a black EOP director might have played a small role in his decision, but mostly he simply did what was best for him and his family. The university soon decided to make the position full-time to better serve students throughout the year, not only the summer. I was in the right place at the right time again, and took the full-time position, a job I would hold for twenty-five years. I plan to be actively involved and committed to the endeavor for the rest of my life.

When I became EOP director in 1971, I already knew from my work the previous summer that I strongly related to the students in the program. I knew what would help their transition to college life—the same academic, social, and cultural activities that would have helped me a few years before. Like most of them I had varying experiences in high school, once failing a history test with a score of 64 (65 was passing) because I got 64 points on the question-and-answer portion, but no points on the essay part of the test. I'm still scratching my head over that one. I remember a teacher commenting in my yearbook about my grades being like a basketball bouncing up and down, though her final comments were that I did have a brain in my head and could do better.

Like many EOP students I was an OK high school student who did not test particularly well, especially on the SATs. There was no SAT test prep in those days—at least not that I knew about. You just broke out a #2 pencil, filled in circles to answer questions, and hoped for the best. Unfortunately, I took the test on a Saturday morning, and we had lost a big game the night before to our rival Francis Lewis High, with first place in the conference on the line. I had played one of my worst high school games, and all that negative emotion carried over the next day and to the exam. That's my story and I'm sticking to it. The idea of taking the SAT again to improve my score never occurred to me, and apparently not to anyone else, either. Besides, that would have been an extra expense that my family didn't need.

In the end, I did have a few college choices. I could have gone to Wharton County Junior College in Texas with my best friend, Jim Gilligan, but my mother put her foot down. Civil Rights Act or no Civil Rights Act, there was no way she would let me move to the Jim Crow South in 1964. That left American University and CCSU. Even with a partial scholarship, American cost significantly more than CCSU, where I got a tuition waiver based on financial need and participation in athletics. I gave up any idea of moving to Washington, DC, and instead headed north to New Britain, Connecticut, where I saw the CCSU campus for the first time. Like most EOP students throughout its history, I hadn't gone on campus tours the way so many kids do nowadays, at least those whose parents can afford such trips. Whatever school I attended, it would have been sight unseen— and I would have benefitted from a program like EOP.

The
Early Years

Part One:
Selecting Students

My give-and-take relationship with George Wyer would guide the operation of the program as we moved forward. I was only twenty-five when I became EOP director, so I knew I still had plenty to learn, but I made a few changes right away that I felt were necessary. Probably the biggest change was adding a writing component to the program. Originally the focus was on math, reading, and study hall—all important elements, and we continued to emphasize them. But I thought learning to write compositions and research papers was also essential for college success, as well as for learning how to think clearly and communicate your ideas in the working world after graduation.

A big question arose immediately: Who would be in the next EOP class, and what would be our best recruiting and selection strategies in the future? It soon became obvious that I would need to cultivate relationships in high schools, particularly with guidance counselors.

From the beginning, I established a pattern of canvasing the state along with fellow Central graduate and fellow New Yorker Dr. Peter Rosa, an assistant director of admissions at the time. CCSU was looking to increase minority enrollment from its current low levels at about 6 percent of the student body (though Connecticut's minority population was nearly 15 percent). Pete being Puerto Rican and me being black, we were a good combination to help recruit minority students. We'd visit high schools—mostly inner-city schools with large minority populations—and meet with students, with Pete talking about regular admissions and me discussing the Educational Opportunity Program summer experience. We found and nurtured relationships with some wonderful high school counselors, like Dick Shepard in Bridgeport, Ed Sudlowski in Hartford, Bob Szymaszek in Meriden, and others throughout the state. I was looking for motivated students with reasonable skill sets who were disadvantaged in some academic areas, or in testing skills, or in focus. In other words, students with potential who did not meet regular admissions criteria. These kids would usually be the first in their family to attend college and, of course, paying for their education was often an issue.

The high school visits took place in the fall, when students were filling out college applications, taking college preparation exams, and exploring their options. We had to juggle our schedules to adapt to schools' visiting times, and there was always competition with other colleges and universities for face time with students. Fridays and Mondays were not good days, and afternoons were even worse, so we tried to condense visits to mornings in the middle of the week. Sometimes that meant getting an early start to make an 8:15 a.m. appointment in Bridgeport or

Stamford. After a while, we learned the back roads to quickly get from one school to another, and hopefully to avoid rush hour traffic. Driving around in those state vehicles, Chevy Chevettes at the time, was not the most comfortable experience, but we got it done. We even had to be careful where we parked. If we had a break between visits and stopped at a supermarket for lunch or a snack (or at a bakery for some of my beloved chocolate chip cookies), people would call and report our license plate as if we were doing something wrong on state time!

When possible, we scheduled our visits to cover several high schools in a town. For example, we would go to Waterbury and hit the three high schools—Kennedy, Wilby, and Crosby. In Stamford it was West Hill, Stamford, and Rippowam; in Bridgeport it was Bassick, Harding and Bridgeport Central. On a typical visit, we would arrive in the morning and go from one school to another, spending about an hour at each before heading to the next school. Sometimes we had to hustle to make the next meeting on time. A lot depended on the number of students who attended the sessions, which could vary from half a dozen to a group of twenty or more.

Prior to our visit, the counselors made announcements and had sign-up sheets for students interested in Central Connecticut State University—or at least supposedly interested. Often there were some kids who just saw an opportunity to get out of class, and at first the counselors would add to the group if numbers were small, maybe so we wouldn't feel we were wasting our time (though we probably were).

Dr. Rosa would begin the presentation talking about Central's programs, cost, location, and criteria for admission. I would follow up with a talk about EOP and how if you did not meet regular admission criteria, you still would have an opportunity to attend Central, but it would entail successfully completing a summer program. I gave interested students a special application. It was essentially the same as the regular application but stamped with the initials "EOP." This ensured that if admissions personnel saw the credentials for admission were not up to standards, they did not reject those students but put them on a list for me to begin the contact and interview process for EOP. In a few cases, an application stamped "EOP" met regular admission standards and was put on the admissions track. In other cases, someone who looked like a good candidate but came up short in an area might be recoded "EOP."

Eventually, the counselors learned what we were looking for and the groups became not only larger but more specific: They were not only interested in Central, but also had knowledge of EOP. It took a couple of years of trial and error to connect with the right guidance counselors, and to have word of mouth from former students filter through the community. At that point, we were able to attract the kind of kids we wanted to the meetings. We had established a reputation in cities like Waterbury, Meriden, Hartford, Stamford, Bridgeport, and of course New Britain, all with high schools that had our target populations. I believe that in every year of EOP's existence, we have had students from New Britain, Waterbury, and Hartford. Our location is ideal for these first-generation students, who are often homebodies with protective parents.

We also went to Northwest Catholic and Hall High Schools in West Hartford (an affluent town adjacent to Hartford), although their minority student populations were minimal. If we had half a dozen come to a meeting, that was a lot. So why did we visit those schools? Hall had a program that bused a few kids in from Hartford as part of a project to educate minority students in the school system. Northwest Catholic had only a handful of minority students, but we wanted to give them an opportunity that they might not have received otherwise. A former softball teammate of mine, Nate Koppel, was a counselor at Hall and would seek out students who were good candidates for EOP. Thus, we did recruit some EOP students from Hall, including Kevin Cranford, whose essay appears later in this book (as do essays by two of Kevin's sons).

The same can be said for a connection at Northwest Catholic who brought several students to EOP over the years, including Henri Alexandre, who went on to become a lawyer, Connecticut's assistant attorney general, and legal director at Connecticut's Department of Emergency Services and Public Protection. Henri's success is particularly satisfying because he was told by a high school counselor that he was not college material, and that he should go to a trade school. We got this one right; EOP worked out for Henri just fine. Sometimes it's not about the numbers but identifying the quality of a student and his or her unseen potential, which I hope is one of EOP's strong suits.

After several years I began to visit high schools on my own, rather than with Pete Rosa. It was more efficient for EOP and the admissions office to focus on our separate target student audiences. We had established great relationships with specific counselors (many of whom had received degrees from Central), and they earmarked the best potential candidates for us. The CCSU admissions staff began to rely more on college fairs and bringing students to campus who were eligible for regular admission.

Meanwhile, I would know what to expect by virtue of contacting specific counselors prior to my visits. By now, those counselors knew that if they had a promising EOP candidate, they could contact me directly and I would take a good look at that student.

I made it clear to students that the EOP application was only the first step, and that a personal interview on campus was required. Potential candidates received a letter to make an appointment for an interview in the spring once their application was complete. That was the first step towards acceptance— making an appointment and showing up on time. Once on campus, students were required to write a spontaneous essay, a paragraph or two about why they were interested in the summer program. This was followed by a one-on-one interview with me—no parents, counselors, or relatives who might have come with the candidate. I would ask a series of questions:

1. How did you get interested in EOP?

2. How do you feel about going to summer school?

3. What are you considering for a major?

4. Where do you see yourself in five years? Ten years?

5. Tell me about your family.

6. Do you have any hobbies or special interests?

7. Any questions for me?

Depending on a student's responses, sometimes I had a follow-up question or two. There were no right answers. I was as interested in *how* they responded as I was in the actual information, which I took into consideration along with their high school record, attendance, and counselor recommendations (some of which held more weight than others, since I knew all of the counselors).

The selection of students to participate in the program was solely my decision. Each summer we accepted fifty students from a couple hundred applicants and more than a hundred interviews. (In 2017, due to increased demand and the initiative of CCSU's president, Dr. Zulma Toro, for the first time in program history the number was increased to seventy-five students.) While accepting students was no guarantee they would attend, we were in constant contact with the students so surprises were rare. We asked for financial aid information, ensured that all forms were filled out, and met with parents and financial aid staff on campus prior to the program's start.

Naturally there were some, shall we say, unique situations—calls from politicians, parents, coaches. Since I was my own man, I had no debts of allegiance that might influence me to take a student less worthy as a favor. Siblings of former students and relatives of program participants did get a "bonus point," if you will, because they knew firsthand what they were signing up for and had the support of prior EOP participants. EOP graduates were our best advertisement. Successful EOP students opened the door for brothers, sisters, other family members, and friends, who now saw higher education as a real possibility rather than some unattainable dream.

In 1988 I had two sisters apply; both had come from Vietnam to Connecticut. One of the sisters, Hongfa Luangkraseuth, was a good candidate, while her sister was not. I accepted Hongfa. She called and wanted to defer to her sister and give her the spot. I appreciated her effort and dedication to her sister but I would not make the exchange. Eventually, Hongfa decided to attend and was quite successful. In fact, she received her teaching degree. Several years later, she was teaching in the same school as my wife, Linda: Jefferson Elementary School in New Britain. She brought her background to the school in dance performances and other cultural events. She was a popular and wonderful teacher. Unfortunately, she had been exposed to Agent Orange during the Vietnam War (called the American War in Vietnam), which eventually cost her her life. A sad day for Jefferson Elementary School and the New Britain school system.

EOP students understood there was no cost for the summer program, and that although participation and completion meant acceptance to CCSU, EOP would not help them with admission to any other school. We always had a waiting list, since occasionally someone would not show on Sunday at orientation. We would attempt to track the student down, and if we had no results by 8 p.m. we would call someone on the waiting list and give them until Monday to arrive. This rarely occurred, and almost always we went with the group that showed up and wanted to be there.

Part Two: Selecting the Teachers

Choosing the right students for EOP was obviously crucial. Maybe less obvious—but even more important—was finding the right teachers for the program. This selection process turned out to be challenging at times. The ideal was to hire professors from Central who were not only fine teachers, but also willing to go the extra mile, who would be available for support and guidance not just in the summer but throughout the academic year.

In my first year as full-time director, half of my job was taken care of because the mathematics section started and developed by George Wyer was working well. His colleagues in the math department were interested and willing EOP teachers. Those professors were exactly what I was looking for, and we continued to hire them year after year.

Unfortunately, staffing the English classes turned out to be more problematic. Complications arose because the English department in the 1970s had a rotating system to designate which professors were eligible to teach classes in the regular summer sessions and which were eligible for EOP. Having received my degree in English from Central, I was quite familiar with the English faculty and had a good feel for those who would connect with EOP students, and provide the skills, passion, and time commitment necessary. I felt other professors were not the right fit for our program. As fate would have it, those were the teachers available. Although it caused some hard feelings, ultimately I went outside the university to find teachers I thought were in the best interest of the program. Most of them were tough, talented high school teachers who were compassionate, committed, and invested in the program and the students.

Initially I sent out evaluation sheets to professors about the students in their classes, a sort of progress report on attendance, performance, and attitude. In some cases the comments were useful and provided good feedback and constructive criticism. In other cases the comments were quite negative, questioning why these students were in the class and questioning their ability to be successful. I quickly eliminated that process so as not to have students labeled by professors and stereotyped as having no chance of success. This also, however, gave me a road map to finding teachers who were compassionate and willing to work with students, and to those who had preconceived notions of students based on their color or background.

As years passed and EOP students graduated from Central—and often earned advanced degrees—half a dozen or more have returned to teach classes for EOP. Obviously, they were familiar with the program and could empathize with the struggles of current students. No one exemplifies this better than Wojciech Kolc, a former EOP student, peer counselor, and resident advisor who has taught EOP math classes since 2008.

I began to add writing and study skills courses, and eventually we required students to take computer skills classes—not a factor in EOP's early years when personal computers only existed in science fiction stories. (At first we didn't even have photocopiers because of the expense; we used ditto machines that created copies in blue ink. I wonder how many people reading this are old enough to remember those!) Over time, course offerings expanded and additional staff were hired. From mathematics teachers to English teachers to the present director, Awilda Reasco, former EOP students continue to perpetuate the success, history, and story of the program.

EOP
Staff

Part One:
In Their Own Words

Meg Leake

In the late 1980s I had to decide between staying in the career education field or transferring to the field of educational opportunity. I had been "on loan" to work with C. J. Jones to operationalize the $3 million grant to establish a Connecticut Collegiate Awareness Program (ConnCAP) at CCSU. I was drawn to the new position, the mission of educational opportunity programming, and working for C. J. We were a good team. It felt right. But was it the right move?

As it turned out, my twelve years with the newly named Educational Support Services Department were the most rewarding of my entire career, and provided the foundation for the creation of The Learning Center at CCSU. So, what made me hesitate to make the move? I was a little nervous about how I would be received by the students. Would they accept a white woman in charge? EOP students were primarily students of color.

I hadn't counted on the man who became my mentor, friend, and partner, Jimmy Knight. He knew I was nervous. His dorm room was on the men's floor, mine on the women's. He assured me that, as long as I was my genuine self, the students would have a positive response. He was welcoming and reassuring from the very first moment. I will never forget the first morning I was to hold a meeting with the students. Jimmy came up to walk with me to the meeting. He took one look at me and said, "You can't wear that dress like that. Go take it off and let me iron it! You'll never make a good impression if you're all wrinkled!"

My nervousness was not entirely misplaced. The students, especially the peer counselors, and I had some bumps along the way that first year. I had to earn their trust. With Jimmy and C. J. in my corner, I found my voice and was able to demonstrate that I really cared about their success. On my thirtieth birthday, at the end of my first year, the students surprised me with a party and a plaque that said, "We love our second mom."

Once I was established as a member of the team, C. J. gave me the autonomy to find new and innovative ways to ramp up students' successes. One of the current trends in education at the time was new research suggesting students learn better if they are taught through their preferred "learning styles." Although that research has since been debunked, we found that helping students think about the way they learned actually helped them focus on their academics. I suspect our success was tied to the fact that we were not asking teachers to teach differently, but were asking students to think about their own learning. We also designed a "learning to learn" curriculum that has stood the test of time. We added a technology course. At the time, not everyone had a computer at home and faculty expected students to be technology savvy!

Reading, writing, and mathematics were staples in the summer program. The curriculum was strong, but the kids were exhausted. One of the things I added to the program was physical fitness, to give them a much-needed energy boost. They also had little time for quiet reflection. I added time for written reflection to the beginning of each study hall. I read them an inspirational quote, usually about resilience, the value of effort, or the power of believing in yourself, then they spent fifteen minutes writing their reflection. At the end of the summer, students turned in an essay describing how their experience in the program affected them. The best essay was chosen and shared at the banquet.

All of the summer staff went their own way at the end of the summer program. I needed to find an efficient and effective way to provide the best possible support and encouragement so that my EOP students would shine academically. The school year was a dramatic change from the structure and rigidity of the summer program. It was too easy to skip classes, fall behind on homework, and struggle with coursework without telling anyone. I needed to take advantage of the camaraderie that had been established and nurtured during the summer. And I needed help!

I created ten groups of five EOP students each who had the exact same courses. They became study groups. They held each other accountable. Each fall I found a big lecture hall class that had two sections taught by the same professor. I registered twenty-five students in each of the sections. This gave me content I needed to teach study skills in a one-credit course called The Master Student. I used what the students were learning in the lecture hall course to introduce them to active collegiate learning strategies, and to teach them to monitor their use of these strategies. Seeing them in class each week helped me keep track of them. It helped me see what they struggled to learn. One thing was very apparent: Math was a huge hurdle. I called the chairperson of the math department and invited the department's math tutors to use our space in the EOP office to provide student support.

I was able to hire a few graduate students to help me. I trained the graduate assistants to facilitate the study groups. Each of the ten EOP groups came to the office each week with their homework. Guided by their graduate assistant, each of the five members of the group worked together to get good grades. They studied, asked questions, reported out their grades, made study schedules, reviewed the requirements of their courses, and sometimes talked through their difficulties.

I also issued a challenge to each summer cohort: Could they get a higher collective grade point average than any other summer group before them? Nobody has ever beaten the 3.1 GPA achieved by the summer class of 1990. We also celebrated all of the students who achieved a 3.00 GPA or better. Grades started to climb with our changes.

I tried to hold every student accountable. I randomly stood outside the big lecture hall class and took attendance. If students skipped meetings, classes, or group, I made them come see me. If they didn't, I went up to the lunch room until they came in to eat and held the meeting over lunch. My students' successes brought me joy. Their struggles brought me worry. My time working with my EOP students was the most rewarding experience of my career. It confirmed for me that every single person, given the right support, can thrive, achieve in the class-room, and achieve in life!

The Learning Center is modeled after everything I learned working for EOP. The Learning Center still hires and trains graduate students who serve the entire campus as Academic Success Coaches. The Learning Center would not exist had it not been for the Educational Opportunity Program.

Lynne Mazadoorian

In 1993 I was provided an educational opportunity that changed my life forever. I had graduated from college with a BA in English a few years before, yet I had no clear vision or career path. I was a hard worker and had quickly risen up the ranks in the service industry. Under the guidance of my grandmother, who was an immigrant and valued education tremendously, I set a goal of becoming a secondary English teacher. I applied to CCSU. Upon acceptance, I was notified of a vacant graduate assistantship in Educational Support Services (ESS) and was offered an interview with Meg Leake. The interview was intense, inspiring, and full of energy. I had never heard so many ideas come from one person. Walking out of the interview, I thought: "I am not sure what just happened, but I want to be a part of this!"

When I received an offer to join the team, I was delighted. Soon after, I began leading study groups, teaching Methods of Inquiry, and helping students find their motivation (or some-times barriers to motivation) through one-on-one learning assistance sessions. Many of the students I served were new freshmen who had just completed the EOP summer program.

These students impressed me daily—they were smart, fun, playful, committed to their educations, proud of EOP, and bonded to each other. I was honored to work with them during their transitional first semesters.

As the assistantship progressed, I realized that I did not want to be a secondary educator; instead, I wanted to work in higher education. I applied for a change of program and was both excited and relieved when accepted into the Counselor Education program. Things began to fall into place. I learned theories of student development and the history of higher education. I learned techniques to enhance my listening as well as questioning skills to support students' cognitive growth and development. I met amazing students who were grateful for the opportunities EOP offered. I built relationships with faculty members who invited me in to their classrooms to share study strategies with first-year students. I was mentored by C. J. Jones and Meg Leake, neither of whom was ever too busy to stop what they were doing and answer my questions (and I had *a lot* of questions). They both tasked me with difficult projects that taught me new skills and increased my competence. They asked a lot from me, because 99 ½ % wouldn't do. Hopefully I delivered.

I learned by observing my peers and colleagues. Montez Johnson, a fellow graduate assistant, frequently modeled how to demonstrate humility, gentleness, and kindness to students while still maintaining high expectations. Camisha Perry modeled a different style—let's just call it "tough love"—by demonstrating she would not settle for anything less than what she *knew* a student was capable of achieving. Awilda Reasco taught me that love always wins. Jimmy Knight showed me that you can keep a sense of humor even in the most challenging moments.

Mrs. Ward taught me that respect matters. Lou Rodriguez demonstrated the power of peer leadership. I learned the most, though, from the hundreds of CCSU students who I had the privilege to meet and know.

My experiences as a graduate assistant in ESS/EOP provided a rich foundation for my career in higher education. I've earned a reputation for being a tough and demanding advocate for students. I suspect that my steadfast commitment to putting students first has been the reason I have been afforded many opportunities to continue to grow and develop professionally. I also believe that's why I've been fortunate enough to have had "a seat at the table" for the planning and implementation phases of a number of exciting initiatives along the way. I thank CCSU and EOP for training me and instilling in me a firm commitment to what matters most—opportunity and success for our students.

Louise Polistena-D'Agosto

EOP was the best teaching and learning experience for me, because of the great leadership of C. J. and the love of all who were (and still are) part of the family who made up the Educational Opportunity Program from 1979–1991, the years that I participated. When I first met C. J., I had been waiting in the outer office, really the large space in DiLoreto Hall before the walls were put up, for about 30 minutes, getting ever more impatient. But as soon as he gave his beautiful smile in that easygoing demeanor of his, and apologized for keeping me waiting, I knew he was the kind of person who cared much for others and for the importance of the mission of EOP. It is because of him (and his prodding) that the program came to be and continues.

I don't think Linda would mind me saying, that C. J. makes you love him and his enthusiasm for EOP.

Over my eleven years with the program, the reunions, my periodic visits, and Christmas cards (not to mention my too-frequent requests for job recommendations!), my respect and admiration for C. J. never wavered. I am ever grateful for the opportunity to have been part of EOP, working with him, and Linda, and the late Jimmy Knight, Meg Leake, Liz Ward, Pete Rogan, Mark Nolan, Vivian Cross, and the wonderful, extremely capable classroom assistants and counselors who made my time there so meaningful: Gail Lewis, Claritza Martinez, Ray McGhee, Loretta Outlaw, Anita Pacheco, Nilda Resto, the late Tony Perry, and others who helped without being asked. I am truly indebted to all of you.

EOP's structure enhanced the experience for us all: hour-and-a-half classes, with teaching assistants who also were counselors to students; mandatory study hours; and excellent activities to develop bonds of friendship as well as learning. Who can forget delivering phone books in blistering summer heat, or the fun car washes to raise money for trips to see Broadway plays? Or all the time and energy and delight in preparing for Mrs. Ward's annual talent show? Or the four nights a week of study hours, working so hard to gain the skills needed for when students transitioned to the future fall/spring semesters? We built a family of support and tension, of struggle and reward, of doubt and confidence, of graduating and moving on to get advanced degrees. I celebrate each and every person for all you have achieved. Being part of EOP enriched my teaching, and more importantly, enriched my life.

A personal highlight I can never forget: It was in C. J.'s old office that I found out I was pregnant with my one and only daughter, Elizabeth, nicknamed "Comma Splice" by Loretta or Gail (I forget who). My wonderful classroom assistants would take my toddler out of the classroom when she fussed and let her play on the grassy areas outside. I had complete trust in them and relied on them to take care of my "precious miracle." I saw them as my own grown daughters. They had my respect from the beginning, each of them so kind, caring, sensitive, and smart.

Though most students came into the program with language or writing challenges, they worked day in and day out, hour after hour, to master college-level writing skills. Not only did they work hard in class; many remained after class for more than an hour for extra help. The purpose of my class was to give EOP students the boost they needed to succeed in regular classes in the fall and future semesters. I remember asking C. J. to get small, black, marbled notebooks, and assigning students to write at least two double-sided pages every night. They were to sustain a topic for as many nights as possible. If they ever played on a baseball team, they could write about a first game, a first out, or even their favorite or least favorite team; anything, actually, as long as it related to a single topic. Why? Because they would have to write five pages or ten pages or longer papers in future courses. I wanted students to realize they have something to say, that they could think in-depth about what they care about.

Besides writing every day there were assigned readings on contemporary issues, because I wanted students to be confident in discussing or writing about social, political, or cultural issues. (This I still do in classes I teach at Tunxis Community College. In the faces of my current students I see the faces of past EOPers).

What I have learned from being part of this wonderful program is that everyone is capable if given the chance, and everyone can succeed if given proper support and encouragement. EOP students I had the privilege to teach have become lawyers, business owners, teachers, principals, and the current director of EOP. I am so proud of being a small part of their success, and to have made a difference.

Part Two: In C. J.'s Words

James Knight

There is only one James Knight, and he is synonymous with the Educational Opportunity Program. Once I became the program director and lived in the dormitory with the students, I knew an assistant was needed not only for my sanity, but the sanity of the students. Enter James Knight.

Jimmy, as he was affectionately known, had entered Central in 1965 and attended classes until he was drafted into the army in 1970. Returning to Central as a student in 1972, Jimmy became quite active and was a founding member of the Ebony Chorale Ensemble. The EBC under his direction became a long-standing group of students who continue to host concerts on campus and represent the university at various events and programs. Often in the evenings during EOP sessions he would be at the piano surrounded by a group of students singing gospel songs. Many of those students ultimately joined the Ebony Chorale Ensemble.

Jimmy was the perfect assistant; the perfect complement for me. He was able to work countless hours during the summer program as well as live on campus during the six-week summer program. Jimmy served as a minister of music at churches in

Waterbury and Meriden. Jimmy was on duty several nights during the week, and when he had choir practice, I was on duty. We would either both be there on weekends, or if he had a church event, or I had a softball tourney (back when I was still competitive), we worked out a schedule that kept us engaged but gave us much-needed breaks.

Jimmy went beyond the call of duty, cooking for students on weekends, helping with homework, directing the counselors. After study hours there were musical sessions to relieve the tensions of the day. Many EOP students became members of the Ebony Chorale Ensemble after the summer program. Jimmy and I created a strong bond of friendship. I eventually became the faculty advisor of the Ebony Chorale Ensemble, a position I held for over fifteen years.

Jimmy introduced me to "99 ½ Won't Do," a gospel song by Hezekiah Walker with lyrics that include, "Lord I'm running, trying to make a hundred, ninety-nine and half won't do." I adopted those words as my life-long theme and began to use it with the EOP students, and later in Athletics. It became my mantra. I had it printed on shirts, hats, business cards, and everything imaginable. In addition to my "99 ½ Won't Do," every EOP student likely heard two phrases from Jimmy that became iconic parts of the program: "Your Mama Ain't Here" and "You Have Plucked My Last Nerve." (Attorney Sonia Owens, EOP 1989, believes she is responsible for Jimmy starting that second phrase!)

Jimmy received the President's Citation in 1975 and was honored by several student organizations. In 2000 Jimmy was awarded the Distinguished Alumni Service Award, the most prestigious of CCSU's alumni awards for service to the organization and prominence in one's career. He graduated from CCSU in 1976 with a bachelor's degree in Music Education and earned his master's degree in 1986.

Coincidentally, the year Jimmy received the DSA, my wife, Linda, was Teacher of the Year at Slade Middle School in New Britain, where they both taught. Jimmy would often bring his young son, Jason, to EOP events, and his daughter, Markesha, was in the EOP class of 1992. She received her degree from CCSU, and Jason graduated from Florida A&M.

Jimmy worked in EOP during the summers from 1972 until 2003. In 2002, Jim developed amyloidosis, a buildup of abnormal protein in organs. It was a difficult year. Having been the best man at his wedding, I felt a part of his family and he of mine. I was able to assist him in his illness to get to his son's graduation before his passing.

I still remember the day he passed away. In the spring of 2003, as CCSU athletics director, I was not having a good day. I decided to go the New Britain Hospital to see Jimmy. He was weak and unable to speak. We made eye contact and I held his hand. He had a smile on his face. I felt good about seeing him and hopefully cheering him up. Later that day, at about 3 p.m. when I went to Slade to pick up Linda, she said, "Why didn't you call to tell me Jimmy passed away?" I was in shock, having just seen Jimmy a couple of hours earlier.

Jim was so loved and appreciated. The auditorium in Slade Middle School, where he so often performed with students, is now named for Jimmy and his fellow music teacher Karl Miller. They died within days of each other, both far too young.

Each year at the EOP banquet, Jimmy would put together a video presentation of that year's program, a tradition that continues today. Jim took countless photos of the students and

events. Those pictures and video will be a major part of the fiftieth anniversary celebration for EOP, bringing back great memories. I know that Jimmy will be with us at our anniversary, especially when we play "99 ½ Won't Do" and "Car Wash," two totally
different songs that are both woven into the fabric of EOP.

Elizabeth Nkonoki-Ward

In 1970, when I began my tenure as program director, I
needed to replace some staff members who had moved on. One
of the first teachers I hired was Elizabeth Nkonoki-Ward. Liz was
from New Britain and had been teaching in the Hartford school
system. Initially she was hired to teach reading during the summer program. Liz spent the next forty years (she recently turned
eighty) with the EOP program. That original course evolved in
so many different directions that "Jack of All Trades" might be
a more appropriate title for it. I gave Liz the freedom to be creative, and she was off and running.

She began by having a party for the students during the
opening days of the session. While a few students may have been
from the same school, most did not know each other. Students
were from high schools throughout the state, from Bridgeport
to Hartford to Waterbury to New Britain, and small towns in-
between. The idea of the party was to get the students to know
each other—so Liz turned it into an assignment! Following the
party, she quizzed the students on the names of fellow classmates and where they were from. It was a wonderful bonding
experience, especially since the students would be facing a tough
summer. Going through it with classmates created many lifelong friendships, and even some marriages.

Liz had a degree in music and used her experience to help students become more confident. Each summer we had a talent show. Each student was required to perform. They could choose anything they wanted but participation was mandatory. Some chose to sing, play instruments, recite poetry, dance, teach a skill, or perform as a model in a fashion show. Some students formed a group and wrote and performed skits. It was a rite of passage to perform. Those activities became part of the EOP tradition, like the annual car wash and trip to a Broadway play.

Liz was responsible for several innovations that became traditions. One of her most significant contributions was the introduction of videotaping. Back in the '70s video cameras were bulky, and we recorded on three-quarter-inch tape and reel-to-reel recorders. As we approach our fiftieth anniversary, those tapes and recordings have become valuable beyond my imagination. At the time I, as well as the students, would often cringe at the sights and sounds caught by the camera. Today I am so thankful we have those tapes. Finding the machine to record and then transfer to DVD was a huge task. I sincerely thank the CCSU media center, Ryan Wark and his staff, and director Chad Valk for making the transformation and cataloging all the tapes and information. Looking back and seeing the students perform is priceless, and makes the fiftieth anniversary a unique, exciting, and memorable experience. I cannot wait to watch the faces of the students as they see themselves twenty, thirty, forty, fifty years ago. There will be laughs, cheers, and joyous memories.

Part of Liz's class evolved into teaching students manners and how to dress appropriately for certain occasions. Any time a guest would enter her class, the students would stand as a gesture of welcoming that person. Fridays were dress-up days, when students had to dress as if they were going to work or to a job interview. We ultimately turned those Fridays into off-campus visitation days. We worked with CCSU's Cooperative Education program staff to have students visit job sites related to their chosen majors and professions; for example, to the local CBS and NBC television studios for those interested in communications. EOP alumnus Pedro Amezquita (winner of the outstanding student award in 1974), was a technician at CBS Channel 3, which made the visits more meaningful. The students could see someone who had been in their shoes, who had made it through the tough summer experience and gone on to graduate from Central, now working in his field of interest and chosen profession. We also visited major corporations in the area, such as Cigna, Travelers, and The Hartford insurance companies, as well as numerous smaller businesses.

A cornerstone of Mrs. Ward's class was to expose students to important individuals who have had an impact on their communities. She had local politicians as guest lecturers in her class. She brought in the mayor of Hartford, and state representatives from New Britain and surrounding towns. She also made a connection with the Tuskegee Airmen, brought them to her class, and helped to get them recognized throughout the state, as several were residents of Connecticut (including Connie Nappier Jr. of New Britain, whose daughter Denise recently stepped down after twenty years as treasurer of the state of Connecticut).

Elizabeth Nkonoki-Ward retired from EOP in 2010 after forty years of dedicated service to the program. I know many students will have stories about her classes as we convene for our fiftieth anniversary. We will certainly have a lot to experience from the visual history documented in videotapes from the '70s, a tradition that continues today—albeit with digital recorders instead of three-quarter-inch tape and Super 8 film!

Jim Meyers

Jim and his wife Sue, along with their two children, Kelly and Eddie, were dorm directors at Central Connecticut in Gallaudet Hall. In the mid-1970s the EOP students were housed, along with me and counseling staff, in Gallaudet Hall for the duration of the summer program. In subsequent years, the program moved from dormitory to dormitory depending on staff assigned for the summer and renovations of various buildings from time to time.

I got to know the Meyers family quite well, and on occasion would find myself in their apartment on the lower floor of the dormitory. One summer, while we enjoyed a glass of wine at their place, Jim started "bloviating" (his word, not mine) about how he could teach my kids. Jim was an English teacher at Conard High School in West Hartford during the academic year. He began describing how he would hold class in the stacks at the library to show EOP students how to write an acceptable college research paper, "etc., etc., blah, blah, blah" (again, his words, not mine!).

I thought it was a tremendous idea and—maybe to Jim's surprise--offered him the job. His previous summer employment had been painting houses and other odd jobs. Jim would later say it was a great decision (despite kidding that because of the wine he might not have been in complete possession of his faculties). "It was never about us," he told me. "It was always about the amazing kids."

Beginning in 1971, Jim spent six years teaching for EOP. Jim joined newcomer Elizabeth Nkonoki-Ward and veteran mathematics instructor Pete Rogan. Jim was into photography and film, so with Mrs. Ward the videotaping and program documentation began. Little did I know how significant that would be. That year at the end-of-session banquet we showed our first Super 8 movie of the program activities, complete with musical accompaniment by Carlos Santana. Jim took videos of some of our cultural trips to see various plays, including *Don't Bother Me, I Can't Cope*; *Raisin*; and *The Wiz*. That footage would be used in various program videos, including the twentieth anniversary video.

The ever-innovative Mrs. Nkonoki-Ward asked Jim to talk to her class about his vasectomy, in conjunction with a visiting lecturer on sexuality. Though it must have been somewhat embarrassing, Jim did a great job answering questions and making the presentation. Sometimes in the afternoons Jim would join me and other staff members in a pickup basketball game against the students. After dinner and during study sessions it was an extra benefit to have Jim right there to assist the students, as he often did.

When Linda and I decided to get married, Central's alumni were sponsoring a trip to Hawaii, so we said, "Why not?" On the Friday prior to the trip on Saturday I opened the door to the courtyard behind the administration building (where my office was at the time). My good friend Howie Dickenman was the best man, Linda's roommate Ellen Stewart was the bridesmaid, and my former roommate George Windish's uncle, Bert Anderson, was the justice of the peace. Jim Meyers photographed the wedding, and the rest is history. Married, cocktails at the Holiday Inn in downtown New Britain, then off to Hawaii.

William Sarmuk

During my undergraduate days at Central Connecticut State University, mathematics was not exactly my strongest subject. I vaguely remember the era of what was called new math. Two plus two did not equal four, and I am not sure how I made it through the class with Professor Belkoe.

When George Wyer drew up the proposal for EOP, mathematics was a major piece of the puzzle. George somehow got professors in the mathematics department engaged in what he was proposing. Since the inception of EOP, excellent math professors have been integral to the program, including Grace Lennon, Narasimbocheri Paduma, Pete Rogan, George Wyer, Mel Pronga, and William Sarmuk.

William Sarmuk brings a combination of detail and humor to the EOP summer experience. He often tells his students that mathematics requires knowledge of basic math properties and facts, and much time in the summer program is spent in those areas. Time is also spent acquiring a positive attitude for learning math and alleviating fear of the subject. Bill encourages students to think like mathematicians, and to enjoy learning. Many "bad jokes" and puns are integrated into his class and the students can't help but laugh, more often at Bill than at his puns or jokes. Bill continues to teach a limited number of courses at Central Connecticut State University.

Bill has taught a number of students who have pursued higher education as a profession. He is extremely proud of those students, who include Oscar Padua and Wojciech Kolc, to name a few. Both were outstanding students, and later EOP counselors and mathematics assistants in Bill's class. Oscar graduated from CCSU in four years, then taught in the Waterbury school system for many years before becoming an administrator in the Hartford school system. He is currently a principal at Bulkeley High School in Hartford. Wojciech has carried the torch even farther, as he now teaches the EOP mathematics class he once sat in.

William has been an integral part of EOP since 1977. He explains that it has been his pleasure to see a positive change within the CCSU mathematics department toward EOP students. The reputation of EOP mathematics students with professors has transformed over the years from fingers-crossed, wishful optimism to expected success. We have this goal for EOP students in all departments in the university. It has been a constant battle over the past fifty years, and is a testament to the perseverance and hard work of EOP staff and students that the program continues to achieve high levels of success.

How They Got to EOP and Where They Are Now

Dimari Flores

Dimari was a smart young lady with a lot of potential. She was a bright star in the ConnCAP (Connecticut Collegiate Awareness and Preparation) program, an offshoot of EOP designed to work with students on academics, study habits, and social skills from the beginning of their high school careers so that by the time they were seniors, their paths to college would be secured.

One summer we held a friendly academic competition with the other newly grant-funded ConnCAP programs at Wesleyan University, Trinity College, and Fairfield University. Our team, led by Dimari and coached by then-director Awilda Reasco, won the competition, the second in a series of summer events between the programs. Attended by all the students in the various programs, it was one of the highlights of the ConnCAP experience.

Dimari not only had the support of Awilda, the ConnCAP coordinator, but her guidance counselor at the high school was Tom Lepito, a friend of mine who I had played softball with and umpired with during the summers. With that team Dimari was a sure-shot, can't-miss student projected for future success on the collegiate level.

But then Dimari lost her way. Unfortunately, it's a story that happens too often. Hanging out with people in general (and guys in particular) who were bad influences, she succumbed to peer pressure and fell off the right track. I was an assistant basketball coach at CCSU as well as the director of EOP, and Dimari's rise and fall reminded me of an experience I had while recruiting a promising athlete. I was in contact with him on a regular basis, establishing a good, positive relationship. Then all of a sudden, when I would try to make contact for our weekly conversation, he was no longer available. It began to trouble me that, whether it was early evening or later at night, he was never home. Eventually he decided not to come to Central, which would have been OK if he had chosen a different school. Instead, some months later he was arrested on serious charges and remains in prison to this day. Dimari did not end up in prison, but she did drop out of high school in 1991. It appeared to be the end of a promising career for a bright, talented young person.

Then, in the fall of 1992, on my way to work, I decided to stop at a CVS to pick up some chocolate chip cookies. I am affectionately (I hope!) known as the Cookie Monster, and often I make a stop to satisfy my cookie cravings. When I reached the checkout counter, the cashier was none other than Dimari! Fortunately for both of us, this was before cell phones so no bystander could record me reading her the riot act. I gave it to her up one side and down the other; I was so mad I might have even cursed. When I finally finished talking about her wasting her talent and potential, I offered her an option to change the path she was on. Get your high school degree, I told her, and I will hold a spot for you in next summer's EOP program. And expect that during those six weeks of EOP the staff and I will be all over you. We will work you hard and you won't have a moment's peace or rest. I gave her my card and finally left CVS.

A few weeks before the start of EOP in the summer of 1993 I got a call from Dimari. She had earned her high school diploma at night school and was now back on track. As promised, I had a spot for her in the program. I did not cut her any slack. She had to fill out an application, go through the interview and writing sample exercises. I had to be sure she was ready to make the commitment.

That summer Dimari was one of the outstanding students in the program, and at the annual banquet she was the first recipient of the Miguel DeJesus Scholarship, honoring her friend and fellow ConnCAP student, Miguel. Dimari went on to get her degree in psychology/criminal justice at CCSU. While she was a candidate for a graduate assistantship, that did not quite work out. She worked in the field for a while before finding her true passion in clothing, makeup, and beauty. After honing her skills at Macy's and Nordstrom, she is presently a makeup artist and fashion merchandiser. She has two daughters, remains active in the community, and continues to support EOP (as well as ConnCAP, until it lost funding in 2017). A few years ago, Dimari spoke at the annual EOP banquet to tell her story.

Nilda Fernandez

In 1985 a young lady from Bulkeley High School in Hartford was a candidate for EOP. She was familiar with the program because in 1983 her cousin, Alfredo Gerena, had attended EOP. In addition, Walt Sadlowski at Bulkeley was one of my go-to counselors. He knew the type of student who needed this program and also had a reasonable chance of success. Based on her record, counselor recommendation, and family support and history, I surmised that she would be a good candidate.

On the day of Nilda's interview, time was running out. I'm a stickler about punctuality and being late does not get you on my good side. About five minutes before her scheduled appearance the phone rang. Nilda was stuck at Westfarms Mall waiting for the next bus to New Britain, which was not scheduled for another half-hour. I was impressed with her decision to call (you had to find a pay phone back then) and sympathized with her for needing to rely on Connecticut's mediocre public transportation system. After all, I grew up in New York with twenty-four-hour access to public transportation.

I got in my car and drove ten minutes to Westfarms Mall. I interviewed Nilda on a bench outside the G. Fox department store and was convinced she was a great candidate for EOP. After the interview she boarded a bus back to Hartford. She was accepted and successfully completed the program.

While Nilda continued her education at the University of Saint Joseph and the University of Connecticut, she got her start at Central Connecticut State University. While most EOP students continue their educations at Central, occasionally some find their niche at other institutions of higher education. Nilda is presently employed at the University of Connecticut Health Center.

John L. Williams

John L. Williams entered EOP in the summer of 1975 from Rippowam High School in Stamford. John L. was an inquisitive and conscientious student who worked hard and took pride in his accomplishments. He had a great personality and was friendly and helpful to others. John L. was also a wrestler and competed on the CCSU team after his enrollment as a full-time student.

I knew John L. would make a great EOP counselor. It has become a tradition to hire former EOP students to work as counselors, because students who had excelled in the summer program understand what it takes and are quite helpful to new students. They have been through it and survived. In addition, they continue to act as mentors during the academic year. Seeing a familiar face and having a relationship with a summer counselor helps in the transition to the regular academic year. John L. was involved in wrestling, became a resident assistant, and for several summers was the face of the summer counselors in the EOP program.

Many lasting friendships are formed in EOP. During the summer of 1975 John L. and Doug Garner became friends, and later both were hired as counselors. They also became friends with Darlene Watson, a counselor in the EOP program, though not a former EOP student. (We also looked for non-EOP CCSU students who would be good counselors and continue as mentors for the academic year.) I had so much confidence and trust in these individuals that when I went on vacation they stayed at my house and took care of my dog. No worries with this outstanding group.

A couple of years later John L., Doug, and David Diagneault from the class of 1977 were in the same industrial technology class, and all of them needed to complete a project. I came up with a suggestion for each and provided materials and resources to help them finish the projects. All of their constructions are still in my house and useful today. Doug made a bookcase, which is in my basement stacked with books, magazines, and other items. David made two deacon's benches lined in cedar, and I store my winter and summer clothes in the chest each season. (Notice I didn't use the plural; unfortunately, the other bench had a run-in with my car in the garage.) John L. made a coffee table from a slab of wood I got from my neighbor who worked at a lumber mill. I have that table in my gazebo in the backyard. The workmanship has stood the test of time, a tribute to the quality of these three people. John L. became an engineer at Boeing; Doug an engineer at Pitney Bowes; and David is teaching and coaching.

When John L. graduated, he had a difficult decision to make. He was offered a job at Boeing in Seattle. Having never been away from home and family, it was daunting to move clear across the country. He took the opportunity and after a long career retired from Boeing in 2017.

While wearing two hats, as EOP director and assistant basketball coach, I began attending the NCAA Final Four and coaches' convention. (I went to every Final Four from 1975 to 2015, and even wrote a book about it, *A Method to March Madness: An Insider's Look at the Final Four.*) The 1984 Final Four was in Seattle. I contacted John L. and he offered his home for my wife Linda and me to stay while we were there for the tournament and convention. Linda, a schoolteacher, was mysteriously sick every year with "March Madness fever" and would usually miss a few days of school, depending on the location of the Final Four. In Seattle we walked by a newsstand and noticed a newspaper with the headline: "Storm in the Northeast. Schools Closed"— for once my wife did not have to take sick days!

John L. is still connected to EOP and maintains contact with several former students who have become lifelong friends. John L. is featured in a video presentation that chronicles EOP's history and some of its students.

Awilda Saavedra Reasco

In 1976 we accepted Elsa Saavedra from New Britain High School into the EOP program. Elsa was one of our best students that summer. We were so impressed by her work habits and personality that we hired her as a counselor for the following year. Keep in mind that even when students prove themselves during the summer, they must continue that process to be considered for a counselor position. We have a tradition of hiring our best and brightest.

In the summer of 1980 Elsa's sister, Awilda, was a student at Prince Technical School in New Britain, working on a skill set for a career in hairdressing. At the time college was not in her plans, but Elsa convinced Awilda to give EOP a try because there were more opportunities for her with a college degree.[2] When Awilda became a candidate for EOP, not only did we know Elsa would support her (Elsa went into teacher education and is presently an elementary school principal in New Britain), but also that Awilda would have a clear understanding of what EOP was like and what it took to be successful.

Awilda worked hard to make herself an outstanding student. Having focused more on job training than academics in high school, she had some catching up to do to prepare herself

2 The Saavedra sisters were not the first set of EOP siblings. That distinction belongs to Phyllis Washington (1973) and her sister Lynn (1978).

for college. But Awilda had a great support system and impressive work habits. She was always willing to learn and help others. After a successful summer and academic year, Awilda was hired as a counselor in the EOP program, a position she held for several years. In fact, one summer she was selected as the outstanding counselor by the students and her peers.

During the school year Awilda was interviewed by the school newspaper, *The Recorder*, and commented that someday she wanted my job as director of the Educational Opportunity Program. At the time I thought that was a nice statement from a former student. Over the ensuing years Awilda and I became quite close. She graduated from Central with a degree in social work, earned an administration degree from the University of Connecticut, and worked for a social service agency.

In 1986 the state of Connecticut allocated money for a new educational initiative: ConnCAP, the Connecticut Collegiate Awareness Preparation Program. The concept was to work with students in junior high and high school to enhance their academic skills and study habits, preparing them for college and creating an educated workforce for Connecticut in the future.

Based on our success with EOP, the university decided to apply for a ConnCAP grant. Dr. Kevin Earls and I put together a grant proposal. We decided to include New Britain and Waterbury because we had strong EOP connections in these communities and they fit the profile for program participants. We were one of several schools to receive a grant, along with Wesleyan University, Fairfield University, Trinity College, and UConn.

The program would be modeled after EOP, with a summer component for participants and attention on math, English, and reading as the base of instruction. The students would commute for the six-week summer session and live on campus the final week of the program. During the school year, staff would be active with parent group sessions and monitoring students' academic progress. Good grades and good behavior were required, and students had to meet performance standards to remain in the program. The goal was to prepare students well for college so that most would not need a post-high school program like EOP to succeed. A major benefit was that students who completed the program would have an automatic acceptance to one of the state universities: Central, Southern, Eastern, or Western Connecticut.

I immediately thought of Awilda as director of the New Britain phase of ConnCAP. I met her for lunch at the Holiday Inn in downtown New Britain to discuss the concept and position. Awilda was interested and ultimately was selected for the position.

In 1995, we partnered with the city of Bristol to submit a grant proposal to the federal government for an Upward Bound program to complement EOP and ConnCAP. Some months later, just as I was moving from EOP after twenty-five years to become athletics director at CCSU, we got word that our proposal had been accepted. That meant CCSU now housed EOP, funded by the university; ConnCAP, funded by the state of Connecticut; and Upward Bound, funded by the federal government. We were likely the only university at the time with three programs of this type intertwined from three different funding sources.

My assistant, Meg Leake, became the director of Education Support Services, the new organization that included all three programs under its umbrella. After several years Meg became the director of The Learning Center at CCSU, a position she held until her retirement in 2017, where she was a pioneer in developing learning styles and methods to enhance student performance. Michael Ansarra, former assistant director of admissions, spent a year as director before joining me in athletics as compliance officer, and ultimately assistant director of athletics.

Then, in 2000, Awilda Saavedra Reasco fulfilled her goal of getting my job. She became director of Educational Support Services (now called Pre-Collegiate and Access Services), a position she holds to this day. Awilda has continued the proud tradition of EOP, while also building on it. Here are some of her innovations:

- Paid internship opportunities with United Health Group Care for EOP sophomores and juniors.

- Partnership with the Travelers Companies. Up to five students accepted into EOP are identified by Travelers and awarded full tuition while they are at CCSU.

- In conjunction with the Confucius Institute at CCSU, a travel program to China. EOP students selected to visit China take once-a-week Chinese culture and language classes.

- EOP has its own math tutors four times a week.

- Governor William A. O'Neill EOP Public Service Scholarships of $1,000 to $2,000 are awarded to approximately twenty incoming students, and renewed if students maintain a GPA of 2.5 or higher.

- Once-a-year community service requirement (students donate items to CCSU›s food pantry and participate in campus events)

- EOP students are part of the Early Academic Warning System, which alerts the director of their academic status if they are in a vulnerable position.

Sonia Owens

Sometimes fate plays a role in the selection of EOP students and it truly becomes the "summer that changed their lives." Take the story of Sonia Owens, a New Britain High School student for whom education was a low priority. Her attendance was sporadic, and her focus on academics, marginal.

The day I visited New Britain High School to make a presentation on EOP, Sonia happened to break her pattern of excessive absence and show up. A counselor making rounds to classrooms was gathering students for the EOP presentation, and Sonia wanted to attend. At the time it might just have been an opportunity to get out of a class for a period, but Sonia saw an opportunity to maybe do something different and not travel down the path she was headed. Based on her grades and attendance, though, she was not optimistic about the prospects of having this opportunity.

I interviewed Sonia, and in spite of her spotty attendance and lack of focus on academics, I had a feeling that she was capable of achieving so much more. That is, after all, what EOP is about. I saw an intangible something in Sonia that was hard to describe, but I knew when someone had it. Her family background and home environment had contributed to some of the issues and problems she experienced. I took a chance on Sonia and accepted her in the Educational Opportunity Program.

Years later, Sonia indicated that at the time she was quite surprised by the acceptance, but looked forward to the opportunity to change the course of her life. During the summer Sonia probably worked harder than she had in her whole high school career. She often stayed up late and got little or no sleep, but she found a way to get it done. Of course, she complained day in and day out about the work required and the torture she was going through!

Longtime summer assistant James Knight seemed to bear the brunt of her frustration. In fact, she is likely responsible for one of the phrases coined by Jimmy that became standard language in the EOP program: "You have plucked my last nerve!"

Sonia was selected Most Outstanding Student of the summer program of 1989. I found out years later that Sonia was more excited by the surprise announcement because her mother, who was in attendance, was able to see her daughter's transformation over the summer that changed her life. Sonia went on to graduate from CCSU, and worked in the community before earning a law degree from the University of Maryland. After working in various law offices, she secured a position as an assistant to the attorney general in Washington, DC. Sonia was an attorney for the US Senate Ethics Committee, but did not find the culture there amenable so left that position. Given her talent and her impressive résumé, I'm sure she has many options for her next job. Maybe one day we will be saying, "Your Honor, Judge Sonia Owens!"

In Their Own Words:
Testimonials from EOP Graduates

Adam Gorski

Dear C. J.,

Thank you for sending a note to me earlier this year regarding the upcoming fiftieth anniversary of the EOP program at CCSU. I often, very pleasantly, recall my EOP time at CCSU. It was a great experience for me and one of the reasons for my success, because I ran into you and you really cared about helping others succeed. I will go through the last thirty years of my life, from the time I arrived in the United States until now, December 2016, so you have enough information to pick from for the EOP story.

Upon finishing mandatory military service during martial law in Poland and receiving a US visa, I moved from Poland on March 20, 1986. It was a hard decision but I saw a great opportunity living in the United States versus Poland. When I arrived in New Britain, I quickly realized that my best option was to go back to school. The problem was with the English language—I could not even say my name in English the way it was pronounced here.

I decided to go to New Britain High School just to learn enough English so I could then go to college. But I would have had to wait until September because the school year was almost over. Not to waste time I enrolled in several ESL classes throughout New Britain, and also found some part-time jobs where I could start learning the language and make a few dollars. In September I started at New Britain High, while still attending a number of ESL classes at night several times per week and working all weekends, holidays, and whenever I had free nights. It was a challenging time for me, but I was lucky to run into Mrs. Rosen, a teacher who worked with students from other countries. Six months later she put me in the "gifted and talented" class, where I managed to improve my English and graduate from New Britain High School in 1988. While in high school I started researching local universities and decided on CCSU due to its close proximity to my residence. Mrs. Rosen suggested that I look into EOP at CCSU, and I am glad I did.

I submitted my application and was accepted. It was a great experience to interact with C. J., his staff, student advisors, and other students over the six-week EOP summer program. We all worked hard, attended the classes, collaborated with one another, and successfully completed the program. EOP gave us great insights into what college student life was and what would be expected from us. Most important, EOP gave us the right tools to succeed as students, find our first real job, and advance our careers. Although it was a hot summer, we all enjoyed being there.

Without EOP, it would have been extremely tough for me to get through the first few semesters at CCSU. EOP gave us an identity and connected us with others. It helped us to fit in and gave us a quick start, putting us ahead of the other freshmen when the first semester started in September 1988. Also, the

EOP office was a valuable place to go for help or get some advice through the rest of our college careers.

While at CCSU I took extra classes (typically six per semester), worked a lot of hours, and got involved with the Karate Club (I've advanced to the fifth-degree black belt so far). After taking so many extra classes, I needed only one class in the second semester of my senior year to graduate. Having a "light" last semester, I decided to get an internship with the Stanley Works (soon to become Stanley Black & Decker), and still graduated in May 1992 with a bachelor's degree in International Management. I wanted to be a full-time student, though, so I took Polish, Russian, and Spanish to have four classes, the minimum full-time load. I also got another part-time job as a dishwasher/cook in New Britain to make enough money to pay my bills.

Upon graduation from CCSU, I felt that I needed more education and enrolled in the MBA program at the University of Hartford while working part-time at Stanley Black & Decker and at the dishwasher/cook job in New Britain. Stanley offered me a full-time job in the sales department, where I advanced to be supervisor of customer service. I kept my other part-time job (on weekends) for about a year.

I had completed my MBA requirements by December 1995 but decided to wait until May 1996 to graduate with my peers. Then, in 1997, Stanley Black & Decker started the Y2K remediation program, and the divisional president asked me to represent the sales and marketing department on that project. I ended up managing a significant part of the Y2K project, with a $15 million budget, for the entire company. That is how I ended up in the information technology (IT) area.

Meanwhile, CCSU contacted me and offered me a part-time teaching position. I ended up teaching required computer classes at CCSU for a year and a half, and also taught at Tunxis Community College one night per week. I really enjoyed working with students but due to my increasing business travels I had to give up teaching (I miss it a lot).

After completion of the Y2K project I was promoted to manager of IT, and worked on a global scale for Stanley Black & Decker until an IT director opportunity presented itself with Inline Plastics. I worked there for five years, then moved to Latex International for two years as their vice president and chief information officer (CIO). In 2007 I decided to advance my career with a larger ($1.2 billion) global company, and became global vice president of IT and CIO with Cookson Electronics. After several mergers, demergers, and acquisitions, Cookson Electronics became Alent, then merged with Platform Specialty Products to became a $4 billion global company. I am currently working on integrating all of the merged and acquired companies worldwide.

Back in 2012, I decided to pursue my PhD in Management with an Information Technology concentration at Walden University. It is an online program and I did most of the work while 30,000 feet in the air (I travel about 70 percent of my time, mostly internationally). I have finished all of my required courses (GPA 4.0), and started my dissertation early in 2016 with a plan to become a PhD by the end of 2017. My goal is to work for another several years after earning a PhD and then start transitioning into a teaching role, first on a part-time basis for a few years, then becoming a full-time instructor. I have not decided which university I would like to teach for, but CCSU is definitely one of my top choices as payback for its opening the window of opportunity for me through EOP and my four-year educational experience.

As with some of the other students we have selected from New Britain, there was no doubt about Adam's academic skills, drive, and desire to be successful. His initial barrier was the English language, since Adam had come from Poland in 1986, only two years before. But Adam was more than up for the challenge, which he proved by being selected as the most outstanding student in the 1988 EOP class.

Henri Alexandre

I was born in Haiti and came to the United States with my family in 1963. When I arrived in Hartford, Connecticut, I did not speak a word of English. I began attending elementary school at Northwest Jones Elementary School, and was set back one grade because of the difference between the school system in Haiti and the United States. (As an aside, legendary Hartford humanitarian Doc Hurley was my gym teacher.)

After two years I transferred to Saint Justin School in Hartford. Upon graduation from Saint Justin in 1968, I attended Weaver High School, one of three public high schools in Hartford. 1968 was a tumultuous year. The Reverend Martin Luther King Jr. was assassinated, and demonstrations for the civil rights movement and against the Vietnam War were common. So many protests occurred during my freshman year at Weaver that I practically spent more time out of class than in class.

Following that year, my father wanted me to transfer to a private school in West Hartford. However, he was unable to afford the tuition because he was raising seven children, and despite working sixteen hours a day did not make enough to afford the additional expense. So at age sixteen I got a part-time job at Saint Francis Hospital as a dietary aide, and worked every day after school from 3:15 a.m. to 8:15 p.m., and on weekends, to pay the tuition. Needless to say, I was not able to take part in any extracurricular activities or sports because I had to work.

Most of the students at the school were white and came from families of doctors, judges, lawyers, accountants, and successful businessmen. Several of the students were chauffeured to school in limousines on occasion. My graduating class had only six black students. At the beginning of the second semester of my senior year, I went to see my guidance counselor to ask for help applying to college. She told me I was not college material, and that I should apply to a trade school to become a plumber or something similar. As a first-generation immigrant and the first in my family to have an opportunity to attend college, I felt dejected. I seriously wondered if she was right, but I was determined to further my education. I did not want to spend my life washing dishes at Saint Francis Hospital.

I decided to go to the admissions office at Central Connecticut State College for assistance. When I arrived, I was sent to meet with Charles "C. J." Jones. That day was the beginning of events that changed my life. C. J. arranged for me to be admitted into the Educational Opportunity Program. EOP was designed to give first-generation college students who are capable of successfully completing a rigorous summer session the opportunity to attend college. EOP guaranteed students who successfully completed the summer program admission into Central, and financial assistance if needed.

I began the EOP program shortly after graduating from high school in June 1972. I found students similar to me who came from across the state of Connecticut, particularly the inner cities. EOP focuses on minority and economically disadvantaged students who would not otherwise attend college. The program began at the end of June and continued until August. The program was staffed with highly dedicated teachers, counselors, alumni of the program, and others, all headed by C. J. acting as a strict and caring parent.

The program was very structured and allowed us to take college-level courses in English and Math and earn credits toward our degree. EOP taught us how to manage our time, how to study effectively, and how to conduct ourselves as college students. EOP also helped us to be self-confident and to set and achieve goals. More importantly, EOP set up an infrastructure of people who would be available to us throughout our college careers to assist us with whatever issues might arise. Lastly, we developed friendships during the summer that would stay with us for our entire time at Central and beyond.

EOP also gave us the opportunity to have fun and experience cultural events that most of us would not have experienced. We were taken to New York City to attend a Broadway play, and we went to Newport, Rhode Island, to experience the Newport Jazz Festival, where I saw Diana Ross perform.

My freshman year at Central was very successful. C. J. continued to meet with every single one of us to monitor our progress and to intervene if necessary. In addition, we had people available to tutor us if we needed help. The friendships we made during the summer also made it easier for us to adjust to campus life during the regular school year.

Following my first year, I moved off campus and took a full-time job at Saint Francis Hospital as a transportation aide, bringing patients to and from the radiology department for radiology procedures. I worked eight hours per day on Monday, Wednesday, Friday, Saturday, and Sunday, and went to classes full-time on Tuesday and Thursday. My first class would begin at 8 a.m. and I would leave Central at about 10 p.m. The lessons on time management I learned while in the EOP program were instrumental in my ability to work and attend classes full-time.

I graduated from Central in 1976 with a degree in Sociology and a minor in Psychology. Following graduation, I continued to work at Saint Francis for another six months, then in January I took a position with the State of Connecticut Judicial Branch as an administrative assistant overseeing the court stenographers throughout the state. This position required me to regularly work closely with judges and lawyers. After about two years, I realized that I was just as smart as those judges and lawyers. I applied to law school and was accepted at several, including the University of Connecticut School of Law. I left my position at the Judicial department and attended law school full-time at UConn. C. J. was one of the persons who wrote a recommendation letter for me to law school.

I graduated from law school in May 1982, successfully passed the bar that fall, and was admitted to practice law in Connecticut. Coincidentally, in November 1982 we had our ten-year reunion at my high school. I had business cards made showing that I was an attorney so I could give one to the guidance counselor who told me I was not college material. Unfortunately, she did not attend the reunion!

Henri went on to have a distinguished career as an attorney, ultimately serving as an assistant attorney general for the state of Connecticut., and as corporation counsel for the city of Hartford. He is currently the legal director at Connecticut's Department of Emergency Services and Public Protections. Henri has also been featured in several EOP publications. He, along with Aida Silva, assistant director of admissions at the University of Connecticut, were on the front cover of an alumni magazine that highlighted a feature on EOP alumni. Henri is quoted in one of the EOP brochures distributed throughout the state: "Tell this year's EOP class it will be worth it in the end!"

Kevin W. Cranford

I am Kevin W. Cranford Sr., EOP class of 1976, and this is my EOP story. Born into poverty in Hartford, I was destined to be a statistic. I was raised in an environment where violence, addiction, and incarceration were commonplace. I am the oldest male of ten children born to my mother. I did not know my father. I look back at my life and realize there were numerous life-changing events that occurred to make me the man I am today.

The first event was being selected for a busing program named Project Concern in the second grade. I began attending classes in neighboring West Hartford, at a suburban school where there were only a handful of students of color. One must note the significance of West Hartford being one of the wealthiest communities in Connecticut, and my city of Hartford being one of the poorest. Going to school in West Hartford caused an interesting dynamic. I did not feel wanted in West Hartford, yet was teased and called "white boy" when I came home. I have not-so-fond memories of running home with my French horn to keep the folks in the 'hood from taking it from me. At the end of every school year I'd beg my mother to let me transfer to Hartford schools. Her response was always, "Baby, West Hartford can offer you a better education and no one can take that from you." She was absolutely correct, God bless her!

Another life-changing event occurred when I tried out for the track and field team during my junior year in high school. I was a better-than-average football player, and a teammate thought I'd be a good track athlete. I showed skill in most sprint events, but I was naturally excellent in the triple jump, eventually becoming a state champion. This success boosted my self-esteem and made me put more effort into my academics.

My senior year I begin to get questions about where I was going to college. I had no idea what college was! No one from my community went to college. When I found out what college meant and how much it cost, I realized my family did not have the ability to fund a college education. Then my third life-changing event occurred. Somehow, the Educational Opportunity Program at Central Connecticut State College was recommended, and I was all in for the summer that would change my life.

In the summer of 1976 I participated in the EOP on the campus of CCSU. EOP was more rigorous than I expected. The work was hard, but through it I gained the tools and support I needed to overcome its challenge. I had a fairly successful freshman year, including athletically, placing second in both New England's indoor and outdoor triple jump. I also placed eighth in the NCAA Division II national meet and sixth in the national under-nineteen track meet.

While running track in the summer of my freshman year I was fortunate to visit a number of different campuses, among them the University of Indiana at Bloomington, Cal Poly Pomona, and the University of Tennessee at Knoxville. During my travels I witnessed black fraternities, and they had a profound impact upon me. As a result, in my sophomore year I decided to become a member of the Omega Psi Phi Fraternity Inc.

Going to school in the suburbs, I did not have many black friends. My only lifelong friend, James Nealy (CCSU class of 1981), was my track teammate and a fellow two-time All-American athlete. I thought being in a large and well known international brotherhood couldn't be bad. Little did I know the pledge process could cause so much hardship. I developed academic problems. I quit the track team and had other negative, self-destructive behaviors that I won't go into. With the help of my mentors and coaches, though, I turned things around and can honestly say that joining this fraternity was another life-changing event for me. Through it all, I've developed friends that will last a lifetime. My two sons, Kevin Jr. (MS) and K'Ronn (MBA), have also become members of Omega Psi Phi Fraternity Inc.

After getting my life back in order I became New England triple jump champion indoors and outdoors. I capped off the year with a fifth-place finish in the NCAA Division II championships, becoming an All-American. In 1981 I was able to repeat as New England triple jump champion indoors and outdoors, and gained my second NCAA Division II All-American honors. I eventually earned my bachelor's degree. It took me longer than most, but I did graduate. In 2001, I received my master's degree from Springfield College. These accomplishments allowed me to encourage my sons to commit to higher education by example.

I'd like to thank the numerous fellow students and faculty who crossed my path at Central. Special thanks go out to

Charles (C. J.) Jones for being a mentor and offering support, especially when I was screwing up. I'd also like to thank my track coaches George Kawecki, John Kelleher, and John Webster—and not only for the excellent coaching/support they gave me. I also observed them in their roles as fathers, and I patterned my parenting skills after theirs. Thank you, coaches.

Finally, I owe so much of who I am to my experiences at Central. EOP set me on a path to become educated and successful. Who knows what would have happened to this little ghetto boy if not for my CCSU education. My life and the lives of my sons have been changed for the better. The lives of their children have been changed for the better. For this I am most appreciative.

Kevin W. Cranford Sr., M.Ed., is retired from the State of Connecticut Department of Children and Families. He was an All-American track athlete in 1980 and 1981. He still holds the CCSU triple jump record over thirty-five years later. In 2006 Kevin was inducted into the CCSU Hall of Fame. He also received the young Alumnus Award from the Alumni Association.

Grace E. Serrano

When I was ten, I had my whole life figured out. I was going to go to college, become an astronaut princess inventor, in that order, and work for NASA. All I needed to do was pick out a school. Around the same time, my sister, six years my senior, was looking at colleges and planning for her own future. My parents took her on a tour of CCSU and I got to tag along. Although the tour was for her, I realized that CCSU was for me.

My mom, Sandy Cruz, went to EOP in 1980, and growing up I heard plenty of stories of all-nighters, outrageous amounts of homework, funny teachers, and delivering phone books on the weekends to raise money. She insisted it was one of the best experiences of her life. I couldn't see how doing so much work in so little time could produce anything of value, except appreciation for sleep.

One evening, she was invited to speak to my cousin's EOP class, the class of 2010. She spoke passionately and highly of the program. She talked at length about how she had learned to manage her time, network with professionals, and live away from her mom for the first time. I was inspired by her words. To me, she had always just been my mom. As I watched her address the tired, soon-to-be college freshmen who hung on her every word, I noticed how happy she looked thinking back to those times, telling her stories, and attributing even the smallest bumps in her college experience to some of the biggest triumphs of her adult life. I was in awe and truly inspired. I wanted to go to EOP and learn everything my mom had learned during her time there.

When it was my turn to be an EOPer, I was beyond excited. After I graduated from high school, I had two weeks to mentally prepare for my new journey. My mom, despite being incredibly nurturing and supportive, didn't give me any warnings or advice. All she said to me was, "It's *a lot* of work but it will be worth it." I was so ready to learn all the amazing skills my mom had learned, which I had completely ignored. To be honest, at the time I didn't think it was going to be *that* much work. In high school, I took five hard classes each day. How hard could three college classes be?

At the end of my first week in EOP, I came home and I cried. I lay down on my bed and cried. I wanted to hug everyone in my house and cry. If I could have hugged my fish, I would have. EOP was far more difficult than I thought it would be, and I came home crying nearly every weekend. However, I knew that without EOP, college would be even harder than that summer looked in the moment. My mom was always there for me, waiting at home with a hug and an "I know it stinks but it's not going to get any easier from here, so keep pushing; you can do it." I kept reminding myself if my mother could do it—without Google, spell check, or online library catalogs, mind you—there was no reason why I couldn't do it. My mother couldn't rely on her mother for help at three in the morning the way I could. I was so grateful and blessed to have someone on my side who had gone through the exact same thing and was doing well as a result.

My mom is now an incredibly successful woman, not only because of the skill set she received in her time in EOP but because of how she remembers it and applies it every day. Many times we learn valuable things and, because we never apply them the way we should, they do nothing to benefit us. I am incredibly grateful to have my mom to look up to and to show me how to apply every day the hard-earned skills I've learned from EOP, the EOP alumni community, and my mother, to continue to better myself and my community. This was indeed a summer that changed my life . . . just like it changed my mom's!

Sandy Cruz was in the EOP program in 1980. She was the roommate of Awilda Saavedra Reasco, the present director of the program. They remain close friends to this day.

Anita Pacheco

My journey to EOP was definitely not one that was planned! It started with a visit by Charles Jones, or C. J. as many call him, to Richard C. Lee High School in New Haven.

Prior to C. J. recruiting at my high school I had never heard of the Educational Opportunity Program. As the sixteen-year-old daughter of a divorced mom who would be the first in her family to attend college, the program was exactly what I needed.

I was not prepared to attend college the traditional way. The application process was painless, but then came the EOP interview. It was the first time I had been on a college campus or been interviewed, and I was terrified. The day I received my EOP acceptance letter was the happiest day of my young life. That hot, long summer was filled with excitement, tears, new friendships, and preparation for my life for the next thirty-five years.

After my experience in EOP I wanted to give back, so I applied to become a counselor my freshman year at Central. I worked for C. J. as an EOP counselor until I graduated, and it was quite possibly the best job I have ever had.

My younger sister Linda saw what a great experience I had, and she too applied and was accepted into the EOP and worked as a ConnCAP (Connecticut Collegiate Awareness and Preparation Program) counselor. Being a part of EOP instilled in me the confidence and academic preparedness to graduate from CCSU with a BA in Communications.

Fast forward to my life as a mother of a beautiful baby boy! From the beginning, I knew I wanted so much for King Edwin Morris III, or Trey, as we call him. Trey was encouraged by his dad and me to give 100 percent in whatever he did. I was a helicopter mom, and Trey knew his road to success would be through hard work and the support of his parents. Trey graduated first in his class, a three-letter athlete who maintained a 4.0 grade point average, all while taking concurrent classes. He now studies at Emporia State University in Kansas, where he plays football and runs track.

If it had not been for EOP and the encouragement of my mentor Charles Jones, I could not have set the road map for my son to be an example of what hard work, determination, and endurance can do. Trey is absolutely prepared to start the next chapter of his life.

Thank you, EOP!!!

Anita Pacheco was in the EOP class of 1984, then became a counselor for the next four years. Two years after she was an EOP student, her sister Linda was in the program, so Anita was a counselor during her sister's tenure. Linda also became a counselor after her summer experience, but with the ConnCAP program, funded through a grant from the state in 1985 with the goal of preparing high school students for college so they did not need EOP-type programs. Anita accidentally broke one of my prized chocolate chip cookie jars. She had a special jar made to replace the one she broke, with chocolate chip cookies all around the jar. I did find the one she broke on eBay some years later. Now every time I look at those two jars, part of my extensive collection of cookie jars with chocolate chips as part of their theme, I fondly think of Anita.

Lorretta L. Outlaw-Satchell

It was the summer of 1986 and I had no clue as to what I was going to do to pursue my education after high school. I did not have many options. I had not prepared to go to college. Although my parents encouraged me to do so, I was delayed by procrastination to apply, or even consider my next move. With no real plan in place, I applied to Central Connecticut State University late and waited for the response. Then the call came: "Would you be interested in attending a summer program that would start to prepare you for college, give you the opportunity to gain some study skills, earn college credit, and allow you to live on campus before your freshman year?"

I said "Yes" on the phone but "Thank God" in my head and in my heart!

I was now a college student, though I never considered how much work this opportunity was going to be. I would float like usual, was my thought—but between program director C. J. Jones, assistant director Jimmy Knight, and Ms. Louise D'Agosto, I was doomed.

Here I was at the Educational Opportunity Program, summer 1986, on the campus of CCSU. My roommate Iris Jones seemed like a sweetheart. We had no problems and our relationship just blossomed. I met her family, she met mine, and together we soared. I am not certain to this day why C. J. and Jimmy would sit outside our door every night. Iris and I just wanted to have some fun! I guess they knew we would leave our room after curfew.

The day-to-day work during EOP was rigorous, but I kept up. I found a balance between work and fun. I enjoyed being on campus, I enjoyed the people, but was this really for me? I knew I could not let my parents down, so I got it done. With the assistance of many, I was successful. I was not stellar, but I had what it took to make it, and I did. I spent many nights rewriting papers that I thought were fine, but they pushed me to be better. The teachers, the counselors, and my peers all pushed. It was like an extended family, and we all wanted to be successful for each other.

After six long weeks, I finished. I graduated from EOP. From this experience I learned to never give up. I learned that there is always a way. I spent many nights studying and working to show that I too was capable. I listened to guest presenters, past students; I observed those I considered the smarter students; and I caught on.

I was now ready to enter my freshman year, with six credits and a definite advantage over the average freshman. Iris and I were roommates and we were ready. I was able to finish my first year with little to no stress. I was good. I knew the campus and a few administrators; I had some friends; so I was all set. At the end of the year, I applied to be an EOP Counselor and to my shock, I was not hired. My ego was devastated. What, C. J.?

"You need a year to mature," he said. "I got you next year."

I went on to my sophomore year and did OK. I finally became an EOP counselor and, just as I imagined it, I was chosen EOP Counselor of the Year! I worked hard to establish relationships, engage the students, and push the principles of the program. It all paid off.

The next year proved to be the same. EOP Counselor of the Year again. Now I was the "woman!" Mission accomplished. I become a resident assistant and moved toward focusing on graduation. I had some academic struggles but nothing was out of my reach for graduation. I had to focus on my residence hall responsibilities, my part-time job, and my classes. I attended my share of parties, but that was all part of the process.

I graduated in May 1990 with a degree in Communications. What would I do with that? I was hired by the state of Connecticut as a classification and program officer. I knew I needed more.

I went on to pursue my master's degree in Counseling, which I received in 1997. I was then promoted to program and services coordinator. Even in the interviewing process I was often reminded of EOP, of Meg Leake and Ms. Nkonoki-Ward. Although I could never be as sharp and poised as them, I always gave it my best shot.

As a result of attending EOP, I gained some lifelong friends: Meg Leake, Larry Hall, Lisa Douglas, Iris Jones, Sonia Downer, Tonya Williams, and Keith Coleman to name just a few, with so many others. They are people I can still count on, and vice versa. Some of them are even godparents to my children.

Today I am married to Larnel Satchell Sr. and we have four amazing children. I am the proud mom of Larnel II and Larnee, and the stepmother of Larnise and Sydney Satchell. We reside in Hartford. Currently Larnel serves as associate pastor and I as a trustee at Mt. Calvary Revival Center in New Haven. What an honor and blessing it is to be able to serve in the Kingdom of God. I am the program and services supervisor at Hartford Juvenile Detention, and am approaching twenty-five years of service with the state of Connecticut. I have a passion for providing services and opportunities to the juveniles detained within the state's facility.

I am grateful for all opportunities afforded to me, and EOP was one of the opportunities that changed my life. I am stronger, wiser, and better equipped as a result of this fine program. I have reached many milestones because of the work and dedication sown into me some years ago. I am a proud graduate of this program and Central Connecticut State University.

Lorretta L. Outlaw-Satchell, M.S., calls herself "the best EOP counselor who ever lived!"

Wojciech Kolc

My name is Wojciech Kolc and I am a proud product of the Educational Opportunity Program class of 2002.

I came to the United States from Poland in 1999 and attended New Britain High School for three years. During my senior year, I knew that I wanted to go to college but I was not sure if I was ready for a four-year college. Everything was new to me and I needed guidance and help. In addition, my SAT scores were low and I did not meet admission requirements to attend CCSU.

During my senior year, my guidance counselor informed me about EOP and recommended that I apply. I do not remember many details but I recall meeting Mr. Pacheco for the first time. He was very informative and encouraging. After a few weeks, I received a letter from EOP stating that I was accepted to the program.

It was a challenging summer. We lived in Beecher Hall and I remember hot days and long study halls. I still remember my counselors, including Jimmy Knight, who was still supervising the evening part of the program. I did not have a chance to get to know him personally, but I learned that he was very respected by students and his coworkers.

During the summer program, I was mentored by Mr. Pacheco and Mrs. Reasco. My teachers were Mrs. Perry, Dr. Kinsella, Mr. Cruz, Dr. Kirby, Mrs. Ward, Mr. Escobar, and Mrs. Blake. They were very demanding but at the same time they cared about each student.

The summer of 2002 changed my life forever. I started believing in myself and gained confidence. I met great mentors. I met people who became my family.

After my sophomore year, I applied and worked for EOP as a peer counselor. I worked closely with Dr. Kinsella. I did that for two years, and during my senior year of college I became a residential assistant for the program.

When I graduated from CCSU (bachelor's degree in Mathematics for Secondary Teachers), I started working at Platt High School in Meriden. One year later, in 2008, I was hired to teach an EOP math section and I continue to teach for EOP every summer. I am also a part-time instructor in the CCSU Mathematics Department, teaching courses in the fall and spring semesters.

Since the summer of 2002, EOP and CCSU have become my second home. I earned my BS and MS in Mathematics from CCSU. I have met many great mentors, including Mr. Pacheco, Mrs. Reasco, and Dr. Kinsella, who believed in me and helped me become who I am today.

I want to thank everyone who supports EOP, including Mr. Jones. This program changed my life, and I am sure that everyone who attended this program would positively share my opinion.

"The summer that will change your life forever!"

Adriene Pitts-Weatherford

Charlie,

In 1979, you took me and many others under your wing in the EOP program and expected nothing but for us to give it our best. Throughout our years at CCSU, you made it attractive to seek nothing less than 3.0 or better. This you believed everyone should strive to accomplish. When we did not meet this standard, you continued to support us.

When we graduated from CCSU, you were there with your camera, voice, and hugs. You made this day memorable. A day to be proud.

When we moved on in life and our careers, you continued to be part of our lives by hosting education seminars, programs, banquets and other inspiring endeavors that kept us close. This provided a chance to return home to show our support and inspire younger brothers and sisters, so that one day they could also be proud. It is as if we have always been your children and you our father. You educationally nourished us, mentally raised us, and physically inspired and employed many of us. You have always given us a reason to also be proud of you.

You were always there to listen to our problems, lift our spirits, understand our needs, and bring joy into our lives. You never complained, screamed, or became frustrated. This is why we were proud of you. We will always love you and what you have done for us.

Janeffer Del Valle

I joined ConnCAP the summer before entering my freshman year at New Britain High School. I believe I was thirteen, going on fourteen. I must say it was the best decision I have ever made for my career (although I didn't realize how important it would be down the road).

Let's just say I joined out of curiosity and to get into a better environment that summer. I grew up in low income housing, my parents struggled financially, and as a teenager there was not much for me to do in my neighborhood unless I wanted to get in trouble. So I joined ConnCAP. Little did I know it would open an unbelievable journey into what was to become my future. I remember the summer classes in the CCSU campus classrooms, and looking forward to joining my friends for lunch in the cafeteria where we got to let off some steam. Most of all I appreciated the Friday field trips when I was able to visit places I'd never been before. Coming from a low income family I'd never been to the beach, Six Flags, the Bronx Zoo, or spent time in the wilderness. Wow—what an experience I will never forget!

I couldn't get enough of ConnCAP so I signed up to join EOP as well. I owe a lot to ConnCAP and the EOP experiences, especially for the friends I met along the way who became an important part of my educational and emotional growth.

I spent time at CCSU even before I joined ConnCAP. I remember as a middle school kid coming to the CCSU cafeteria, where my Dad worked, wondering what it would be like to study at CCSU. Where would I start? Would I be eligible? Would I be good enough to get in? Well, thanks to my dear C. J. and my dear Awilda Reasco, I was in. ConnCAP motivated me to push hard and pursue a college career. Once I was in EOP, that just made my college experience even more worthwhile since I started with a great GPA. I had never worked so hard in a summer month for school, but EOP motivated me to do so and gave me the right tools I needed to succeed.

Thanks to the EOP experience I was able to strengthen my writing skills and humbly accept the Miguel DeJesus Scholarship award, which helped me get a start on my first semester's college tuition. Receiving this scholarship was a special honor since I had the pleasure of knowing my friend Miguel through school and ConnCAP. I know he will never be forgotten.

Both ConnCAP and EOP gave me opportunities to get a college career I wouldn't have received elsewhere. I completed both my bachelor's and master's degrees at CCSU. I now have a beautiful family and a career I can't get enough of. Thank you, C. J. and Awilda, for believing in me and for opening the door to an amazing college career. Dreams do come true!

James Nealy Jr.

I am delighted to be allowed to submit this short appreciation letter concerning the EOP family. Although I did not attend the program directly, I have always felt a kinship to EOP and I owe a great deal to the program and its members. Without my EOP family I would not have had the opportunity to become a corrections officer, a Connecticut state trooper, the director of school police and security, or presently the assistant chief of public safety. I am and will forever be very thankful for the support and direction that I received during my EOP/CCSU experience.

During the summer of 1976 my best friend Kevin Cranford asked me to come up to CCSU for a visit. He had been attending EOP. I had never been on a college campus other than to participate in a track meet. Although I was a sought-after high school track and field athlete, I really had no intentions of going to college or participating in sports past high school. I had planned on enlisting in the Marine Corps after graduating from high school in 1977, but that all changed when I visited the EOP session during the summer of 1976.

I was amazed at the level of organization, direction, concern, focus, and drive that I observed in the summer students as well as the teachers, most notably Mrs. Nkonoki-Ward, who

I am still great friends with. I felt an amazing atmosphere of support, high expectations, and care. I also heard things from the students that changed my focus. They spoke about plans to become teachers, lawyers, bankers, and computer programmers. No one in my immediate family had gone to college and I had never heard anyone speak in this manner. At this moment my focus changed and I decided that I would try my hand at college.

I felt that if I could get accepted at CCSU, the support system that I had observed could and would spill over to me as I navigated through college. At this point in my life, I felt a kinship to EOP, and I applied to CCSU. I was admitted, thankfully, some months later. As Kevin Cranford's roommate, I had a constant connection to EOP through him, for which I will forever be grateful.

While attending CCSU I decided that I wanted to be a police officer. I was fortunate to have been guided and encouraged by you, Mr. Rosa, Mr. Floyd, Mr. Martin, and the awesome choir director, Mr. Jimmy Knight, as well as by other members of the EOP organization. I also was able to observe the interactions of professional men in a professional setting. This was all new to me and very, very empowering. I suddenly knew how success looked from an up close and personal perspective.

I had my first real job while attending CCSU. Coach Bill Detrick hired me to videotape the games of the basketball team. I learned a great deal from him as well. He would always say to me, "I have a job for you, Jimi, if you need one." I appreciated his kindness. My track coaches were also very supportive and made me feel like they valued me as a person. I am very grateful to have had coach Kelleher, as well as coaches Kawecki and Webster, guiding and supporting me through my collegiate journey.

They always reminded me that if I couldn't talk to them, then I should seek you out when trouble was around, and I did on a few occasions. You always were a vehicle to get me refocused, as I did slip up a few times. Without the EOP exposure, I am certain that my life would have turned out very different.

I made some lifelong friends while at CCSU and most are EOP alumni/friends who have supported and encouraged me through the years, an ongoing support network that was born and sustained because of my EOP affiliation.

While attending CCSU I also observed that it was the EOP students who were the leaders about campus. Everyone looked to them for guidance and inspiration. They always reached out to assist with study skills, tutoring, career advice, and direction. What an amazing group of students, who I felt were ahead of their time and who I believed were our future leaders. I was inspired by them, so much so that I got involved in college life by joining organizations, attending choir practice, starting a poetry club and a book club, deejaying, and lending a helping hand to others.

Over the past several years I have been returning to CCSU to participate in the annual alumni "Making Connections" event. I share with future CCSU professionals the tools that they will need to be successful in today's world. The tools of success that I share are the same ones that were shared with me by the EOP staff, students, and administrators. They are timeless because they work, and they have allowed me to live out my professional dreams.

In ending I say with the deepest appreciation, thanks to you and to the many EOP members all about the country. Thank you all for sharing the EOP experience with me.

Annabelle Diaz

I found out about EOP through my high school guidance counselor during my senior year. My guidance counselor saw the potential in me, potential that I did not see in myself since I had no interest or goals for my future, let alone attending college. I knew that I wanted to live a better life . . . I just did not know how, and felt that I did not have the tools to succeed since I grew up in poverty. My guidance counselor informed me about EOP, and told me that I would be a great candidate for the program since he knew that I had the drive and intrinsic fortitude to survive. He felt that all I needed was an opportunity, a change in my environment.

Following our conversation, I viewed EOP as the passport toward a life-changing experience. I slowly started to think differently about my future. I applied myself and as a result, I graduated salutatorian of my class in 1997. As I addressed the crowd at graduation in June 1997, I felt an overwhelming feeling of self-worth and empowerment. I then craved this feeling, and I planned for short and long-term goals. I was addicted to accomplishing and achieving my goals and dreams. I was eager for the opportunity that EOP had in store for me. I was curious about learning, but even more important was the exposure I was going to have to a completely different world from mine. This was my one-way ticket to a desired destination . . . EOP.

Although I felt ready for the experience, I was terrified inside. It was the first time away from my home, my family, and my neighborhood. Fear tried to paralyze my judgment and willingness to learn on many occasions in the EOP classrooms. These insecurities hindered my every thought, especially when I felt unworthy of sitting in a university classroom. I was able to overcome this fear in EOP by establishing relationships with mentors. I created connections and found that I was not the only one struggling academically or experiencing a powerful urge to give up and return to what I knew, what felt comfortable to me . . . my neighborhood, my friends. EOP taught me grit! It taught me perseverance and tenacity, essential elements in who I am today.

I will never forget the summer that changed my life *forever*! After my EOP experience, I felt comfortable and accepted at CCSU. I felt a sense of relief knowing that I had friends and mentors who would support my journey at the university. This is why today, I am a triple CCSU graduate. I have my BS and MS in Educational Leadership, and doctorate in Educational Leadership from CCSU. I decided to dedicate my mission to education because I also want to "pay it forward." I am currently a school principal at an urban high school in Hartford. My goal is to positively influence and inspire the masses, as a community leader. I am a steward of positive societal change, in no small part thanks to EOP.

Ron B. Glass

Ron B. Glass III is an EOP alumnus from the class of 2004. He, like many of the students, often wonders how he got there. He got there because of hard work, tears, and the overwhelming thought of the college experience, which most EOPers are not familiar with. They have no idea what to expect or how to adjust to an experience where they will be on their own and ultimately responsible for their future. Once Ron made that commitment to the EOP program, as he says, "I was in it to win it."

His father and grandmother were his caretakers. In high school he had no direction or clue what path he should take. The question was: Should I go to work or make an attempt at college? While he had good grades and was recognized for his achievements, he felt college was not for him. His mentors, Jackie Bethea and Latonia Kendricks, informed him about EOP, and he followed through with the process for acceptance. The interview process was filled with anxiety. Being shy, he had to sell himself as a worthy participant.

Next came the waiting game to see if he made the grade, always the hardest part for the candidates, especially when everyone around you is optimistic but you yourself are not sure. He finally received his acceptance letter as one of the fifty students selected to attend EOP in 2004.

Naturally, Ron had mixed feelings about the times adults, on one hand, told him he could do something with his life, while others told him he would never amount to anything. At that moment he was angry, but looking back he appreciated the motivation on both sides of the spectrum. During EOP he did what every student has done since the program began in 1969. He described it as "I cried, I laughed, I pulled all-nighters, I studied, and I failed." He recalls one particular evening in particular. Students were having a group debate, something he could never do because he was scared to be in front of people. When it was his turn, although nervous, he walked to the mic, looked around very quiet, stood there for a minute, then busted out crying and left the room. A couple of fellow EOPers came out to see if he was OK. The motivation at the time was powerful. He can remember them saying, "You can do it; if you could not, you wouldn't be here." One peer in particular told him, "I will stand by your side while you do your debate." After thanking them, he smiled and went back in to complete his part of the debate. It was the first time he felt good about himself in front of strangers. It was the beginning of great friendships. He met some amazing people in the process, including his mentors for life, program director Awilda Reasco and assistant director Harry Pacheco. They saw potential that he did not see in himself. He was, and is, extremely thankful for that.

After graduation, Ron B. Glass continues to give back to EOP. He established a scholarship in his name to give four students each year $1,000 and a plaque—truly a wonderful gesture from a former student.

In 2016 at the Annual Alumni Awards Program, Ron B. Glass was recognized and awarded the "Young Alumnus Award" for his accomplishment after graduation and his continued support of the EOP Program. As Ron puts it, "I can honestly say the EOP changed my life." Ron is constantly busy and is developing a clothing line: He presently has snapback dad hats and winter caps; T-shirts with short and long sleeves; and sleeveless vests. Who knows—maybe Ron will produce some items for the fiftieth anniversary.

Ron is a self-proclaimed workaholic and presently holds down several jobs. He works at the Humanidad group home full-time, at the Two Rivers Magnet Middle School as a substitute teacher and mentor, and at the Village (whose mission is "to build a community of strong, healthy families who protect and nurture children") on a per diem basis.

As unique as ever, Ron was the only EOP alumnus to write his story in the third person!

EOP
Funding

The Educational Opportunity Program has been funded by Central Connecticut State University for the past fifty years, and I anticipate continued funding for the foreseeable future. Each year at the EOP banquet I encourage that year's group to strive for excellence and success as they determine the fate of future classes. In the early years, before significant increases in minority enrollment, the EOP with fifty new students annually was the basis of the minority population at CCSU—even the relatively few minorities not in the program were thought to be participants. We were constantly under the microscope so it was important to be successful.

The program's survival started with President F. Don James, when the program began, and has continued through Dr. John Shumaker, Dr. Richard Judd, Dr. Jack Miller, and now Dr. Zulma Toro, the first female and first minority president of Central Connecticut State University. Dr. Toro has already shown her commitment to the program by expanding its numbers from approximately fifty students to seventy-five (with a transitional class of sixty-four in 2017–2018). She has increased funding for the larger numbers and has allocated additional scholarship money to support the students. Dr. Toro is also playing a significant role in EOP's fiftieth anniversary celebration by hosting a reception for returning students and staff the day before the reunion banquet.

Because of CCSU's institutional support, EOP has an enviable tradition of unbroken service that separates it from some other programs. Federally funded Upward Bound, for example, is an excellent program but is contingent on applying for a grant every few years, and there is no guarantee that your institution will receive funding in the next cycle. In some cases programs receive funding for decades, only to eventually lose their grants for one reason or another. Unfortunately, this happened at both Trinity College in Hartford and Wesleyan University in Middletown, when their long-time Upward Bound programs did not have their grants renewed. The schools did not choose to continue to support the programs through college funds, and thus the programs were eliminated. Similarly, the high school program ConnCAP lost its state funding in 2017 and is being phased out despite its history of success.

EOP Scholarships

Several years after being hired at Boeing and moving to Seattle, John L. Williams sent a check to help other students in the Educational Opportunity Program. I credit this generous action by John L. with starting the EOP Scholarship Fund.

The EOP Scholarship Fund is strictly an endowed fund, which means that the principal remains untouched and only the interest generated can be used to pay for scholarships. It is a supplemental fund, in a separate account from the operating budget that pays for staff, books, and related program activities. Supplemental funds are where donations can be made for various activities like trips, cultural events, luncheons, and other activities that are important to the EOP experience but not budget-line items.

Since that initial check John L. has continued to send donations, and many, many others have followed his example. For the twenty-fifth anniversary I set a goal of $50,000 for the scholarship fund. A successful phone-a-thon conducted by former EOP students, teachers, counselors, and friends of the program played a major role in getting us near the $50,000 mark. By the night of the twenty-fifth anniversary banquet, in October 1993, we were only $2,000 short of the goal. I made a pledge that night of $1,000, and alumni director Nick Pettinico and CCSU trustee Harry Mazadoorian (whose daughter Lynn later worked for EOP as a graduate assistant) made pledges that brought us to $50,000.

From that point we continued to set our sights higher, and the endowment slowly but steadily grew. By 2015 it had reached $700,000. At the annual banquet I usually give an update on the scholarship fund, and that year I decided to totally go for broke (actually it's the exact opposite of going broke, but you know what I mean). I told the crowd that our new goal was something completely unthinkable not so long ago: a million dollars in the endowment by EOP's fiftieth anniversary. It's great to think big, but I knew hitting that figure wouldn't be easy. The fiftieth anniversary was only three years away, which meant we needed to average $100,000 in annual donations to reach the goal, a daunting task.

They say it's better to be lucky than good, and I like to think EOP is both. Not long after the banquet I went to lunch with my friend Nick Pettinico, who was now executive director of the CCSU Foundation. Nick and I go to lunch a couple of times a year to catch up on things, and one of those things is an update on the scholarship fund. We were at J Timothy's in Plainville when Nick handed me a paper with the latest numbers. I was hoping that we had edged a bit farther over the $700,000 mark.

I nearly fell off my chair. The new total was over $950,000!

It felt surreal. I can't remember if I actually said something to Nick, or if the shock on my face was question enough, but he explained that Costco had donated $250,000 to the fund. In one stroke, the huge challenge of raising $300,000 had become a completely manageable $50,000. So we set a new goal: to push as far as we could past $1,000,000.

I'm happy and proud to announce that because of the generosity of so many, as of this writing the Educational Support Services Scholarship Fund (as it is now known) stands at $1,126,432, a figure that will definitely rise by the time of the fiftieth anniversary banquet on June 30, 2018. Approximately $32,000 in scholarships were awarded during the 2017–2018 fiscal year, a significant jump over the $19,000 given out in 2015. Before long, helped by the magic of compound interest as our endowment increases, we hope to be providing annual scholarships that meet or even exceed the entire $50,000 endowment in 1993.

The scholarships are designed to help a nice cross-section of participants pay their CCSU bills. Every year the most outstanding student in the summer program is honored, as selected by the teachers, counselors, and the director. Since the program had a significant number of Black and Hispanic students, we established that an EOP student active in their respective student organizations, the Black Student Union and the Union of Puerto Rican Students (now the Latin American Student Organization), and in good academic standing, would receive scholarship money. I then focused on the most successful students in the various summer courses: math, English, reading, critical thinking, etc. These scholarships were often named for people important to EOP's development, such as longtime assistant director James Knight and former counselor Tony Penny (both of whom died far too young), and art professor Al Martin, a champion of students in general and minority issues in particular. As the fund grew, we began to give scholarships to an outstanding former EOP student from each class: freshman, sophomore, junior, and senior. For a few years the state agreed to match donations, a dollar for every two invested, but it rapidly fell behind, and the program was discontinued with money still owed, and surely never to be paid.

Scholarships named for outstanding (and generous) individuals are granted every year, including Miguel DeJesus, Ron Glass, Scott Pioli, and Bill Bumpus. Community organizations and businesses that identify with EOP's goals have established scholarships in their names, including the Travelers, Costco, Ronald F. Gilrain (from the Community Foundation of Greater New Britain), Alvin B. Wood, the Koteen Family, the Vincent Foundation, and Governor William A. O'Neill, to name just a few. CCSU academic schools, seeking to attract and encourage minority participation in their disciplines, have also become part of the scholarship program. (What a huge change from the dismissive attitude toward EOP that some at CCSU had when the program was first established.) All of these are in addition to the scholarships provided by the endowment.

The CCSU Alumni Association has also been a great help. Over the past few years they designated $100,000 to "double-dare" Central alumni and supporters to donate to CCSU programs, with the association matching those donations (up to $1,000 per individual). Naturally Linda and I each donated $1,000 to get the number to $4,000. I got on Facebook and the phone and encouraged other EOP folks to break out their checkbooks, leading to $10,500 in donations, for a total. with the match, of $21,000 for the scholarship fund.

EOP has come so far financially from the early years, when at the annual banquet we just handed out trophies and certificates. Recognition for students' accomplishments is great but help with tuition costs is definitely a welcome addition!

Car Washes

After talking about an endowed scholarship of over a million dollars, it might seem strange to end this chapter with a section on car washes. In fact, though, for the first twenty-five years or more of EOP, annual car washes helped us fund cultural events for the students, especially trips to New York to see Broadway plays. (We also raised some money delivering telephone books, occasionally chased by a dog or two.)

Many EOP students had not been out of their neighborhoods, let alone the state, and fewer still had been to Manhattan. Virtually none had seen a Broadway play. It's one thing to hear about these things, but to experience them formed memories that last for lifetimes. For example, *West Side Story* is one of my favorite plays, and we not only saw it in the theater, we visited several New York locations where scenes from the movie had been filmed.

The car washes were generally on campus behind the student center, though once or twice we washed cars at Saint Francis of Assisi Catholic Church on Stanley Street near the university. We began around 10 a.m., to get that first group of students coming out of summer classes. We placed students at strategic locations, waving signs and yelling "Car wash!" (Usually the female students—pure marketing.) As hard as it might be to imagine today, with CCSU's much more insular campus (a huge improvement), at that time Wells Street was a main road right through the middle of the campus, running from New Britain to Newington, so it wasn't just students we were trying to attract, it was lots of people from the community driving by. We made friends with the maintenance and housekeeping personnel on campus, in particular Dino Muratori and Catherine Vieira, and they provided us with buckets, vacuums, rags, soap, hoses, and most materials we needed to go along with our manpower.

It was always a fun-filled, tiring day. The EOP kids worked in shifts; while one group was in class, the others washed cars for the morning sessions. After lunch, all hands were on deck. We stopped at 4 p.m., after the last daytime summer classes. The students would then go to dinner and begin study hour at 6 p.m., as usual.

After a while we became experts, and in addition to the signs and live action we placed notes on cars while students were in class. One summer, just as we were about to begin, a campus police officer came to me and said because of a drought New Britain had put a ban on watering lawns and washing cars. Total bummer. We had to pack everything up, take the notes off the cars, and send the students to class. I went to see the Dean of Student Affairs at the time, Dr. R. L. Judd, who would eventually become president of the university. He understood the importance of the team-building exercise as well as the accomplishment of students contributing to their cultural experience. Dr. Judd allocated some funds to make up for our lost income so that we could attend a Broadway play that year.

The car washes created a sense of teamwork among the students, and pride that their efforts were contributing to their extracurricular activities. Not to mention the fun they had, washing cars, dancing to music (including our theme song for the event, Rose Royce's 1976 disco hit "Car Wash"), and in the end spraying each other when Jimmy Knight and I gave up the hose!

By the late 1980s, however, the EOP car washes had faded into history. Ticket prices for Broadway plays had become exorbitant, rising even faster than the cost of college tuition, which is saying something. We had always managed to get by, helped by generous rates from DATTCO bus company and group discounts at the theaters. (When necessary, the staff chipped in as well.) Eventually, though, new economic realities took over and EOP simply didn't have enough money to continue the tradition.

Bumps
in the Road

Due in part to our extensive screening process, once students arrive on campus for the summer program there is a very high completion rate. Still, it's fairly common for a couple of students to get homesick and threaten to leave. On that first weekend when students go home, we wait with some doubt about a select few who might not make it back for Sunday study hall at 8 p.m.

In the early years of the program, students could earn up to six college credits. Three were an elective reading class and three were in mathematics, depending on their skill level and what they learned during the summer. They would test into the appropriate level math course like any other freshman. Even today, EOP students take the placement tests for mathematics and English to see which level course they can register for, ranging from remedial courses to upper level mathematics courses, depending on their major.

In the first couple of years a handful of students did not earn any credits, subsequently did not successfully complete the EOP program, and were not able to attend Central in the fall. Students had to pass at least one of the credit courses to be allowed to register. In those rare cases, we did not embarrass the students and allowed them to go to the closing ceremonies. In those cases, we advised the students to explore a community college in their hometown area, in hopes that they learned a valuable lesson from the summer experience. It was my job to inform these students of their status, which kept the results private so very few people had any knowledge that a particular individual would not be joining the freshman class that year.

Then there was the case of two young ladies from Hartford, who were friends from the same high school and did not take the summer program seriously at all. In the first week, they were often late for class and negligent in completing their homework assignments. Generally speaking, by week two everyone has an idea of what is expected and the counselors are up in the wee hours of the mornings helping those who need help to catch up and get back on task.

These two were having none of that. The backbreaker for me was when, one day, they were not in class. When I found out, I hopped into my Volkswagen camper and drove to the dormitories on the other side of campus. I found them in their room and informed them that I was done with them—pack your bags and call home to have someone pick you up. I was so mad, I hit the back fender on my Volkswagen bus as I backed up to leave.

Too late, the ladies realized the opportunity that they had and how they had thrown it away. They contacted their guidance counselor, who in turn contacted Dean of Student Affairs Dr. Richard L. Judd, who later became president of the university. He had to make sure that due process had taken place before the dismissal. In the final analysis, Dr. Judd upheld my decision and the girls were dismissed. I often thought that if they had worked half as hard while they were in the program as they did to try to get reinstated, things certainly would have turned out different for them.

At the 2017 banquet and award program, as a student was receiving a scholarship for his success in one of the classes, director Awilda Reasco commented, "You wanted to go home the first week." It could only bring a smile to his face—to everyone's face, actually. Like so many other EOP students who had a tough time at first, he had stuck it out and reaped the rewards. That summer had definitely changed his life.

The big concern for the EOP class of 2017, at sixty-four students our largest group to date, is that financial necessity will require some of them to continue working part-time jobs and live at home to help defray the cost of their education. College costs have risen dramatically, and state support for higher education has dropped. In prior years, a combination of loans, scholarships, and federal grants based on need allowed almost all EOP graduates to live on campus, which kept them in close touch with the staff, counselors, and classmates, and made it easier to keep everyone on the right track. When a first-generation student has to work, especially early in their college career when they most need emotional support and to learn academic discipline, it is not a great formula for success.

Miguel DeJesus

Miguel DeJesus had been a student in the ConnCAP program at New Britain High School for four years and planned to attend Southern Connecticut State University after graduation.

He was greatly looking forward to it. In hindsight, I suspect that Miguel chose SCSU in New Haven over Central because he wanted to get away from gang involvement in his community and begin a new chapter in his life.

Awilda Reasco was the ConnCAP director at the time. She selected Miguel for the program and was his advisor and mentor during his years at New Britain High. She also created bonds with the parents of the ConnCAP students and kept them engaged through activities such as parent meetings, fund-raising events, college visits, and assistance with applications and financial aid forms.

One day during the 1993 ConnCAP summer program, Miguel asked me if I would talk to a group of students, which I agreed to do. Awilda and I had recently learned of his involvement in a gang, but Miguel was intent on improving his life and was an advocate for others. We met at the Newman House adjacent to the CCSU campus. About a dozen young people showed up, both male and female. I spoke to them about the importance of higher education, and the opportunity to continue their education beyond high school via programs like ConnCAP and EOP. I wanted to give them hope and direction. I'm sure Miguel was looking to show them that there was a better road ahead if they chose to take it. Miguel had written an impressive essay about young people in New Britain having nothing to do, which ultimately could lead to involvement in gangs, not only for friendship and companionship, but also as protection against crime.

We did not know how heavily Miguel was involved with the Latin Kings gang, but unfortunately it must have been significant because one November morning on his way to school, Miguel was shot and killed in the New Britain High parking lot. Shock does not begin to explain Awilda's and my reaction when we heard what had happened. I spent several terrible days giving interviews to various news outlets, often reading excerpts from Miguel's essay on the plight of students in the New Britain community. It was a real challenge to keep my voice from shaking.

His parents, and particularly his mother, who had built a bond with Awilda and the program, to this day continue to hold fundraisers every year, via bus trips, bake sales, and other events, to provide for a scholarship in Miguel's name. The scholarship is given to a student from New Britain who attends CCSU, and is renewable annually. Although Miguel's mother attends the banquet every year to present the award, it never seems to get any easier. I can see the pain and anguish in her face as the winner is announced and comes up to receive the award. She constantly struggles to hold back the tears. But her son's memory lives on for the good he was trying to do. Though we lost him, Miguel has had a positive effect on so many others, and that influence will continue well into the future.

Here is Miguel's essay, written as part of a ConnCAP English assignment:

The End of Innocence

The end of innocence is here. No more do we hear about not saying this or that in front of this kid, because nowadays the kids know more than we do. They don't know the academics, but they know the streets, and they think that's all they need to know. They're wrong but they don't realize that. They think if they beat some other little kid up, or steal a bike, they think that's how they gain respect. I don't blame them for thinking like that, because that's what they learn from their peers, and parents. If you know nothing else other than drugs and violence, then that's all you do. It's all about morals, which are not your fault, but society tends to blame the fruit instead of the person who planted the seed.

The innocence is gone. Never again will kids be able to go outside and not be exposed to drugs, hunger, or to poverty. The youth of today have nothing to do. They have no place to go. Especially here in New Britain, it's dead out here. We don't even have a movie theater. Then you wonder why we have so many gangs out here. If you have nowhere to go and nothing to do you feel alone, and when you feel alone you need to belong to something. When we have nothing to do, some of us turn to drugs and alcohol. It helps us forget we have nothing to do. It relieves our problems, but on the other hand, it causes more problems, because some of us get violent when we drink or do drugs. Therefore, when we do it and expose the kids to this way of life, they no longer can call themselves innocent, because at an early age they become a part of the problem, and the innocence is gone.

These kids do not grow up happy, because they know no happiness. How can you expect to learn how to be happy from people who don't know happiness themselves? Happiness in the streets is to be able to survive another day. Being able to leave your house and come back safely is happiness to us. Leaving the house and coming back to find all your furniture and TV is happiness to us. That's how we lose our innocence, we don't care about nobody, just ourselves. In the street nobody cares if you've eaten, or if you have a place to stay. They don't care if you're mentally ill. Because they don't care, they have no time for sympathy, for nobody has sympathy for them.

The next generation is going to be very hardcore. Just think about it, you have babies having babies. The sad part about it is that these kids are not born healthy, some are born addicts. Some are addicted to dope, cocaine, and alcohol. This is not their fault, but that's the way it goes when innocence is lost.

—*Miguel DeJesus*

The Next Generation:

Letters from Children of EOP Graduates

I wasn't sure what the title of this chapter should be. I first thought I might call it the "Kids of EOP," but that would be misleading because it's less about the kids of EOP than the *parents* of the kids of EOP, and how their experience in the "Summer That Changed Their Lives" set the course to change the lives of their children. These children are not the first in the family to attend college, and had the ways, means, and resources via their parents to pursue higher education and enter into any profession they want. They have the tools, desire, and goals to go beyond their parents' dreams.

Then I thought maybe we should call this chapter "The Next Generation." In reality, that is what they are: the next generation in the family tree. Fortunately for this generation, their parents made choices that helped provide a clearer path for their success. At the core of that path is education. Their parents struggled and made sacrifices that put them in a better position to provide for their children, who now have huge advantages and can pass these advantages on to *their* children—the third generation in this cycle, and counting.

Then I thought, maybe we should call this chapter "Not EOP." The parents who completed EOP ensured that their children would be on a path to improved skills and increased focus on education, so that from an early age their goals and aspirations were set at a high level that required sound educational preparation. As a result, the post-EOP generation has matriculated at dozens of colleges and universities, including Harvard, Cornell, UConn, Hampton, Arizona State University— and, of course, Central Connecticut, where it all started. They were well prepared for higher education, and most had no need for summer programs like EOP.

The remainder of this chapter includes testimonials from students whose parents attended EOP. You will see why I struggled to give this chapter a title, because I think these stories cross all the categories: kids, generations, and "Not EOP"!

Timothy Diaz-Jalbert

Banana leaves and guanábana trees. Stray cats in the yard and small lizards in the kitchen. Tobacco farms, Sunday church service, and the mating call of the coquí. Sharing a small home with seven siblings and a bedroom with two sisters. These are just some defining characteristics of my mother's childhood, having grown up on the winding roads and farmlands of the mountains in Matón, Puerto Rico. Born to a Pentecostal Christian minister and a hard-working traditional mother, she and her siblings were raised with no more than the bare necessities. The sisters and brothers shared everything from their wardrobes to their Christmas presents, and finishing the food on your dinner plate was never optional.

My mother seldom calls attention to, nor seeks credit for, the humble beginnings from which she grew and matured. However, her origins should come as no surprise for a woman with such brazen character and strong faith that she accomplished paving a path to success for herself while remaining deeply rooted in family and her faith in God.

After moving to the US mainland with her siblings and parents, she started to learn English in middle school, and graduated from Guilford High School. Without Central Connecticut State University's Educational Opportunity Program, my mother may never have had a viable opportunity to pursue education beyond this point. Thanks to this summer program, she was accepted to CCSU the following August, despite underwhelming academic credentials that stemmed in part from her struggle to study a high school curriculum and perform well on the SAT with a language barrier. She was able to work full time to pay for her undergraduate degree, and would later return to CCSU for her master's in Spanish literature. She was immediately hired as an adjunct Spanish professor at CCSU and has since become the department head of foreign languages at St. Paul Catholic High School.

My mother has never stopped encouraging me and my siblings to aim extremely high, even in our most difficult and least confident times. She has always had much higher expectations of us than we ever had of ourselves, because she was blessed with a means to break society's perception of her academic potential. It was almost exclusively her encouragement, insight, and optimism that gave me the audacity at sixteen years old to apply to one of the most challenging undergraduate universities in the world, Cornell, where I recently completed my degree in Neurobiology and Behavior, leading to my acceptance at the University of Cincinnati and University of Connecticut medical schools.

Her talent and passion for teaching also inspired my sister Jessica to follow in her footsteps: Jessica recently graduated from Fairfield University's Five-Year Education Program to become a certified elementary school teacher. Our youngest sister Julianne has dreams of becoming a veterinarian, and it can't be a coincidence that her study habits and grades have greatly improved since surviving our mother's freshman Spanish class last year!

My mother has achieved great things, but her story is far from over. Each day she continues to inspire her family, colleagues, and students with her dedication to scholarship, family, community, and faith. She continues to share her wisdom, to lead as a living example that hard work and discipline are necessary for success and happiness, and to demonstrate that it is always important to recognize the blessings that open the door for your good work ethic to bring you to your destination. For her, the Educational Opportunity Program was among the greatest of those blessings and helped direct her down the path to becoming the scholar, professional, and life coach that I am proud to call my mother.

Noemi Diaz-Jalbert was from Guilford, a town with a very small minority population. Several Guilford students had preceded Noemi to EOP, including Olga Felix and Luis Perez, showing that when you have success with an initial student or two, word travels and you are able to attract other capable students. Noemi's EOP class of 1984 was particularly strong, with six students going on to be counselors in future EOP sessions.

K'Ronn W. Cranford

My father, Kevin W. Cranford Sr., grew up in inner-city Hartford during the '60s and '70s. During this time Hartford was a city stricken by poverty, racial unrest, and limited opportunities for education and career advancement. To quote my father, "It was the 'hood."

Moving forward almost sixty years from his birth in 1958, something amazing has happened: little Kevin Cranford, a tall, stringy, tenacious youth, has become the patriarch in his family. We can determine that all of his successes come from one blessed opportunity: In 1976 the Educational Opportunity Program was the entrance for my father to attend college, and because of this my life was forever changed.

My dad often talks of being part of a social project that bussed inner-city youth from Hartford to suburban West Hartford. While he was afforded the opportunity to learn, he was also introduced to stark racism. Oftentimes he would spend an entire school day where no one would even take the time to talk to him, no one knew his name. Moving forward with bravery, courage, and aspiration on display, my dad entered the Educational Opportunity Program. It changed the lives of my family.

While attending Central Connecticut State University, my father was twice NCAA All-American in track and field, and was initiated into the Omega Psi Phi Fraternity Inc. Shortly afterward my dad met his future wife, my mom. They ventured into the diverse world beyond the ghetto. My father often reminisces about how he was presented with blessing after blessing, but that shouldn't overshadow his work ethic. Building on his collegiate success, he started a family, and in 1985 my big brother Kevin Jr. was born.

"I don't want you to be me. I want you to grow up and be better than me," were his frequent words. Beyond his financial and emotional support, my father's worldly experiences gave our family a blueprint of what life could be. We soon saw our aunts and uncles move out of Hartford and into Manchester, East Hartford, and South Windsor in search of education and opportunity for their own families.

When I think back, I realize how much the EOP program has given my brother and me. As I write this letter I am days away from moving to Hawaii. Each and every turn my life takes, my dad has been behind me, encouraging, prodding, and reminding me of the man I came from. I too have walked in his footsteps. I received a full ride to Morgan State University, earning my BS in Marketing, before attending SUNY Binghamton University for my MBA. My father's scholastic and athletic legacy was always something I was determined to advance on. Did I mention he is in the CCSU Athletic Hall of Fame? Now my nephew, Kevin III, has every opportunity to build on his grandfather's legacy.

My father came from the most humble of beginnings. Due to his tenacity and aspiration, mixed with blessings (Project Concern, EOP, etc.), he has changed the lives of his family. Without this opportunity my dad had every chance to succumb to the Beast of Poverty. I want to thank my father and those at the EOP because I would not be where I am today, eyes forward, looking to the islands, if it weren't for all of the hard work they and my father put in for the past fifty years.

K'Ronn W. Cranford, BS, MBA, works in senior business analysis and attended Morgan State University and SUNY at Binghamton University.

Kevin W. Cranford Jr.

When considering what my father's college education means to my brother and me, I immediately think of where we'd be without it. Growing up in inner-city Hartford with a single mother who had only a partial high school education, college was an unlikely destination for my father or his nine siblings. With the soft bigotry of low expectations it's easy to imagine our father, like many others with similar upbringings, getting trapped in the inner-city cycle of poverty. If the apple doesn't fall far from the tree, what would that have meant for me? The outlook and prospects for my life would be drastically different from their current realities.

If my father hadn't been exposed to higher education and achieved in college, he most likely wouldn't have met and married our mother. Herself a product of the Hartford school system, she too was fortunate enough to attend college and earn a degree. In looking for suitable partners it was surely important to our mother that any potential mate have credentials that matched hers. If it weren't for college my father would have been relegated to a different end of the dating pool, never getting a chance to swim by our mother.

But fortunately for me and my brother, our father did attend college and earn a degree, thereby creating opportunities previously unimaginable from his inner-city upbringing. He was able to meet students and faculty from diverse backgrounds, travel the country through his talents on the track, and challenge himself academically through the rigors of college coursework. This widened our father's perspectives of life's possibilities. He wouldn't be trapped in the inner-city cycle of poverty. He would attain his piece of the American Dream and enjoy the upward mobility that education offers. His future family would have a firm footing in society as a result of his earning a college degree.

When I think about what my father's college education means to me, I focus on what an outstanding role model and example he has been for my brother and me. Without his drive for education, my brother K'Ronn and I likely wouldn't have earned our bachelor's and master's degrees. If it hadn't been for the Educational Opportunity Program for first-generation college students, my father would never have been exposed to what college has to offer. EOP transformed the trajectory of our family. Now, two generations later, we look toward the future, and fully expect my son, Kevin W. Cranford III, to be the third generation of Cranfords to attend college.

Kevin W. Cranford Jr. earned his BA and MS at Morgan State University.

Ilhan Braxton

If I were to say all the ways my mom has influenced me, and everything she has sacrificed for me, I would be here all day. My mom has wanted nothing more than my success and happiness, and it's because of the sacrifices she has made that I am living my dream of going to college. It's because of her influence that I now have my degree from UMass Amherst, graduating a year early. My determination and ambition to achieve my goals in life sprouted in elementary school, but it wasn't until middle and high school that they blossomed. This is because of my mom's choice to send me to a school in a completely different town.

At the time, going to Capital Prep was my version of torture. I thought my mom was punishing me by separating me from my best friend and sending me to a school that was year-round, starting in July. Now I see that it's because of this choice that I learned the discipline required of me in the future. Being surrounded by like-minded people challenged and motivated me. My mom knew that by staying in New Britain, the only challenge I would face would be reaching my full potential in a school system that was failing its students by not caring enough. She wanted more for me, and that's what she gave me.

Being in a school that focused on college readiness and social justice taught me to work hard and question the world I live in. It taught me that as a woman of color, I would need to fight to succeed in a world that did not think of me as equal. My teachers taught us that in life there will always be those who doubt us, and that all they're doing is challenging us to prove them wrong. I now see that my mom's choice to put me in an environment full of people who wanted to help me succeed was the best decision she's made (besides having me, of course!).

Now that I'm in college I look back on my mom's constant nagging to get my homework done first, and I can't help but laugh. It's because of that nagging that now my first instinct is to get my work done first before doing anything else. When I question myself I always think WWMD (What Would Mom Do?) and it usually elicits some form of motivational saying. Her positivity stays with me, and her love keeps me going through the hard times. Like finals week.

I don't think I would have made it this far without my mom's constant support. I face every challenge, and ten-page essay, with the grace and positive mentality she has bestowed upon me, and I welcome any haters because all they do is show me I'm doing something right (another lesson from my beautiful mother). All I know is, when I have children of my own, I can only hope to live up to bar she has set. But it's because of her that I know I'll face that challenge head-on and succeed.

Ilhan Braxton is the daughter of Dimari Flores. Dimari was in both ConnCAP and EOP. Her story is in a previous chapter in the book; now you have a connection, and maybe a better understanding of why she did what she did for her daughter's welfare.

Gabrielle Julia Bachoo

My mother, Aida Silva, has been an inspiration to me for as long as I can remember. As the first in our family to graduate from college, she opened the door for all of us to move on to bigger things, inspiring education and innovation throughout the younger generations. By going to college, she secured an amazing job in undergraduate admissions at the University of Connecticut. She now not only helps our family, but people from across the world whose dream is to go to college.

None of this would have been possible without the EOP program. As a young woman whose first language wasn't English, EOP gave her insight into the difficulty she would face once the full semester began. Taking classes to improve her English, as well as learning how to study and speak to professors, enabled her to graduate and have a community that would help her through the many struggles.

My mother's perseverance led to a domino effect within our family. Now I am a sophomore at UConn and the majority of my cousins have gone to college, which has led to great things for all of us. We have been able to join the work force, create homes for our families as my mother once did for all of us, and live our dreams as she did. My mother's trip through higher education and her current job in higher education allow her to give us real knowledge about what we can do in and out of school, and I am thankful every day that such an amazing woman raised me.

Aida Silva was in the EOP class of 1982, one of the best EOP groups. She is presently associate director of undergraduate admissions at the University of Connecticut.

Ashlee J. Williams

Every day since I can remember I have heard my father tell me, "My goal in life is for you to pass me in education." For so long I wasn't sure of what that would mean for my future. I never thought of myself as a person who would be in college. But as my parents said, I never really had a choice but to go. I saw my dad pull out his diploma many times, but not until it was my time did that piece of paper have so much meaning to me.

I didn't physically see my father go through all his trials and tribulations when he went through school. He always instilled in my brother and me that education is power. "Without knowledge, you don't have anything. In this world, they can take any and everything from you, but one thing they can never take is the knowledge you have." This statement stays with me even now, at the age of twenty-six.

I can't imagine being where I am today without my dad being a college graduate himself. Seeing him do all he did with an education was amazing. He wasn't only there to show me the importance of education, he also showed kids he mentored in Black Achievers (a national program run through the YMCA), and even the kids he coached. He told me and my cousins any chance he got that we should get an education—that it didn't matter what it was for, or even if you changed your mind about where you wanted to go in life, because you had that degree as a backup plan if you needed it, and you had the ability to say, "I did that." You accomplished it, and you experienced something that not everyone is able to do. He encouraged so many people to do great things and inspired me to want to reach the goal of passing him. I wanted to be able to tell my children the same thing.

I saw how successful my father was and how hard he worked to be able to accomplish all the things he had done, things that I wanted to do in my future. What also really inspired me was seeing my mom going to college. I went with her to class, and sat with her, and got to experience firsthand what it was like. I got to read books with her and experience the culture of college, and even though the experience didn't include everything that college is made up of, it made a huge contribution to how I looked at higher education. It changed my whole view of what school was about. I loved the whole concept. I got excited to be involved, to hear educated conversations. To be a part of a higher learning community was amazing. I saw her working on her homework and creating things; having her read this whole new world of ideas was so exciting. From then on, I knew I wanted to go to school and grasp all the knowledge that I could.

Both of my parents have had an enormous impact on my views of a college education and its great importance, especially as a young woman of color. I saw how important it is to have knowledge, and to be able to use that knowledge to be anyone I wanted to be. Because of that I enrolled in community college, and after two years decided that I wanted to expand to a university. Arizona State University is where I chose to go, and it was the best decision of my life. This school gave me a chance to be away from home, and to grow and learn things about myself and about the world. It was the best three years of my life and I became an ASU alumna in May 2014.

College not only gave me book education, it gave me life skills and confidence in myself. Without my dad's words of wisdom and seeing my mom in school I may have taken a different path. I'm currently working on my master's degree at Seattle University to become a school counselor, with plans to next obtain my PhD, thus reaching the goal of passing my father in education—as he always wanted me to do.

John L. Williams II

I grew up in a house with two siblings, and my parents always stressed how important education was for our future. It was at the forefront of every family conversation. My parents stressed the importance of keeping our grades up, not just for any incentives, but for the sole purpose of understanding what it means to be educated and having something that is yours.

While we were in high school, extracurricular activities were also important in our household. Everything we did had a purpose in building our résumés for entering college: YMCA computer programs, Bible school, summer camp, reading programs, and participating in sports like football, basketball, softball, bowling, golf, and track and field. Clubs, fundraisers, running tournaments—you name it and I was a part of it somehow.

My father, John L. Williams, often quoted my grandmother, Anna C. Williams: "Education is the one thing no one can take away from you!" My father would always tell me stories, and the one that really stuck out for me was the one about "the summer that changed my life." He was given a chance to go to college, but first had to attend the Educational Opportunity Program for six weeks during the summer! Later, he made it his priority to ensure that my mom fulfilled her dreams by returning to college, and to have my sister and me witness and internalize her accomplishments, so that we would set our goals to do the same and further our education.

My parents expressed to all of us that college was something we should strive to attend and graduate from as one of our life goals. In my early teenage years, during middle school, I had the chance to attend labs, classes, and visit my mother's campus, and to see her graduate not once but twice. She decided after twenty years to go back to community college and complete two degrees, then transfer to Seattle University to receive her undergraduate degree. She followed that by earning her master's in teaching.

Both of my parents, especially my father, were clever in their approach to our education. He even put my wonderful godparents into my life. Both of them had college degrees, and they made it part of their responsibility to make sure we went to college, to graduate and succeed in life. My godparents have two beautiful daughters, my godsisters, who are older than my sister and me. Seeing them both go to undergrad and graduate school, and further educate themselves, just made it more intriguing for us to want to do the same.

Despite these excellent role models, when it was my time to attend college I did not know where to go, or even what I needed to go for, outside of wanting to play football. The first couple of schools I went to were only to play football, until I finally realized that college had more to offer than sports. I decided early in September 2012 to transfer from a college in North Carolina to Arizona State University. The only things I knew about ASU were that it was very big and my older sister was going there at the time. Not until I attended a few Justice and History classes, which really piqued my interest, did I get a good feel for what was expected of me. Those classes became the determining factor for me changing my major and figuring out what was best for me.

My father and sister helped in the decision, simply by telling me, "Study what you like." This is when I got into Interdisciplinary Studies. I knew from my classes that history and justice studies were topics I was interested in, and interdisciplinary studies allowed me to integrate both.

Throughout the rest of my years at Arizona State, I sometimes let frustrations get the best of me. I remember calling my father in my last semester and having long conversations with him. His final words to me at the end of each conversation were, "Son, just finish strong!" To this day, I remember to "finish strong" in everything I do. The day I told him that I was on track to graduate, all I could feel was joy! Education was now not only important to my parents, godparents, godsisters, and siblings, education had become important to me. Everything I put into learning became about understanding the world we live in and how to make it a better place. The key to it all is education.

Kayla Reasco

My mother has always taught me that you should always work your hardest and try your hardest, no matter the little (or no) resources you have, or the obstacles that may be in your way. There are never excuses.

When I was growing up, both of my parents worked *really* hard to make sure that I had everything I needed, *and* more. In our household, my mother would come home late from working eight-plus-hour days, while my father (who is the best cook I know) had dinner prepared for both her and me. Gender roles were never "a thing" for me growing up. I was raised to become a strong woman, by both a strong woman and a strong man. My parents both taught me that if my heart was in the right place, I could do anything I wanted to do.

I start by sharing this because my mother's work ethic and passion for helping students (who were once like her) came from the values of EOP and the mentors she met along her journey—C. J. Jones being one of them, even to this day. My mother went through EOP in 1980; a year later she became an EOP counselor, then associate director of EOP, and finally director of Precollegiate and Access Services. Talk about a woman who gets what she wants. She knew what she was saying when she told C. J., as an EOP student, that she wanted his job one day—and she got it. I'll let C. J. tell that story, though!

EOP influenced my mom to not only work hard, but to take everything that she learned and use it to help others. There's a famous quote: "True leaders don't create followers, they create more leaders." I can say with confidence that my mom has twenty-five-plus years of tirelessly working to help inner-city students across Connecticut receive a higher education, become amazing leaders, and become our future.

Thank you, Mom, for always showing me the importance of not only doing well for oneself, but the importance of *giving back*. And for teaching me that not all jobs are done within the hours of 9 to 5!

Raishaun McGhee

Education has been an important aspect of my life since the very beginning. Having two college graduates as parents helped set the academic standard in terms of the path I would take that would lead to a college diploma.

I guess you can say my academic journey began before I was even born in 1988. That summer my dad (Ray McGhee) attended the Educational Opportunity Program at Central Connecticut State University. When I was growing up, he explained to me how that program changed his life in terms of helping him truly value the importance of education and preparing him for the academic challenges ahead of him. Both he and my mom (Venice Ross), who also attended CCSU, communicated to me early on about how vital it was to set a high academic standard for myself and to never shy away from educational challenges or opportunities. Having these two as mentors left no room for doubt or uncertainty when it came to applying for college and continuing my education after high school. My environment at home had a strong impact on creating my own academic goals and beginning to envision the path I would take.

One of the biggest obstacles that I had to overcome on my academic journey was the switch from public to private school. I grew up in Windsor, Connecticut, attending both elementary and middle school there before making the switch to Rye Country Day School to continue my education. It was difficult for me to leave behind childhood friends and teammates, but my parents knew what was best in terms of setting me up for academic success and giving me the best opportunity to attend a prestigious university after high school.

Another significant challenge for me was the culture shock. I went from being in a predominantly African-American school system to being the only African-American male in my entire class. Dealing with this change was no easy feat; however, I knew that I was there to get an education, and I persevered to take advantage of the unique opportunity in front of me.

My parents' decision to have me attend Rye Country Day School changed my life drastically. This ultimately led to me receiving an offer to play football and get an education at Harvard University, one of the most prestigious academic institutions in the world. My parents' guidance, and their constantly stressing the importance of education, helped me reach this achievement. That, along with my ability to embrace change and willingness to adjust to whatever the circumstances may be has led to my success, and also has helped me mature into the man I am today.

Things are not always going to be comfortable, or ideal, but what truly matters is how you approach the situation and what you get out of it. Everything should be treated as a learning experience. Being able to experience two different educational settings, both culturally and academically, truly opened my eyes and prepared me for not only college, but also for the real world.

Harvard was an amazing experience. Some of my highlights include attending lectures given by some of the world's most renowned professors, winning three Ivy League football titles, cross-registering at MIT's Sloan Business School, listening to Mark Zuckerberg and Joe Biden speak at commencement—the list goes on and on. My four years in Cambridge flew by, and I created relationships with roommates, teammates, professors, and coaches that will certainly last a lifetime.

I am fortunate enough to have received a full-time job offer at an investment bank on Wall Street, and I am extremely excited to start this next chapter. As I continue on my journey, it is, and always has been, important to stay true to myself, remember where I started, and continue to be a role model for those younger than me, starting with my younger brother. With the state of race relations and uncertain political and social conditions in this world, it is important for minorities to continue to strive for greatness and set the bar high in absolutely everything that we do, to experience success and to pave the way for those in the next generation.

Rena Jenkins

From an early age, my parents instilled in me the importance of education. No matter what activity or event I had coming up, school always came first. They pushed me to be at the top of every category in class, from AR points in elementary school to AP classes in high school. My parents stressed that being serious about my education would only benefit me in the long run.

Being a three-sport athlete in high school gave me the opportunity to hone my time management and organizational skills early on. I always knew that my homework and assignments needed to be completed prior to practices, games, and team events. My mom, Patricia Baldwin Jenkins, was a student-athlete in high school as well, so she knew how much time and dedication went into being a student first and an athlete second. She always went the extra mile to make sure I had the best tools to succeed. With my mom's constant encouragement and support, I was able to graduate high school at the top of my class with high honors.

I am now in my third year at the University of Georgia, pursing a bachelor's degree in Management.

My mom's inspirations of years ago are still evident today in my educational path. Both my parents have bachelor's degrees, but my mom went a step further and also received a master's degree. This opened many doors for her and helped her to become the successful woman that she is today. I aspire to one day find a suitable program so I can follow in her footsteps and receive a master's degree as well. Her success inspires me day after day to push myself and make the most out of my time.

My mom positively affected me daily and had a major impact on my life. I pray to have her determination, perseverance, and heart. She has shown me that with faith and hard work you can accomplish anything.

Rena Jenkins is the daughter of Patricia Baldwin Jenkins. Patricia Baldwin was the outstanding student of the EOP class of 1978 and later went on to be a counselor. She graduated from CCSU in 1982.

Renaldo Jenkins

In the Jenkins household education was always a top priority. From a very early age I remember my parents stressing the importance of working hard in the classroom. My mother, Patricia Baldwin Jenkins, encouraged us to read one hour each night prior to bed. One day Mom said, "Choose an instrument. Music stimulates your brain academically." I took trumpet and piano lessons from middle school through high school at her request. She would always make sure that all of my homework was completed before I was allowed to participate in any extra-curricular activities. I watched my mom juggle family, work, and worship. Time management was crucial, and being so busy I soon learned to emulate her organizational skills.

I grew up loving sports (football, basketball, track, karate, and baseball), and she truly made sure I understood the importance of a student athlete. She clearly emphasized that I was a student first and an athlete second. These life lessons opened doors and created a smooth transition for me in several areas. My mother's work ethic spilled out into me and was noticed by college and professional scouts who came calling. Thanks to my mother, my academic achievements were just as notable as my athletic abilities.

I always admired both of my parents for having college degrees and wanted to follow in that path of excellence. Coming out of high school I was granted the amazing opportunity to play professional baseball. My mom's inspiration and guidance led me to see the value in continuing my education. I promised my mother that I would continue my education no matter the outcome of my professional baseball career. I kept that promise by attaining an associate's degree in Business online while playing baseball.

I am currently working toward a bachelor's degree in Risk Management at the University of Georgia. I've had some challenges; it takes courage to attend college after a four-year break. All those years of Mom's unconditional love, faith, discipline, and perseverance kicked in. In hindsight, I am truly blessed that my mom, who was also a student athlete (volleyball, softball, basketball, bowling, and track) instilled consistent hard work into me at a young age and encouraged me to take my education seriously. It is preparing me for my future endeavors and has proven beneficial for my life choices.

My mom inspired me as a young child, and to this day continues to encourage me to be the best I can be. I'm inspired by my mom, who was partly shaped due to her collegiate experiences at Central Connecticut State University. Thank you EOP for the start of my mom's college education. She received her bachelor's degree in Accounting and continued on to receive her master's in Business Education.

I thank my biggest cheerleader for her support in the decisions I make and for being an example of how you can do well in school as well as in life.

Renaldo M. Jenkins II is the son of Patricia Baldwin Jenkins, CCSU 1982, EOP 1978.

Graduation

College graduation is a milestone event for all students and their families, but I think for EOP participants it's even more special. It certainly is for me, thinking back to the summer when the students began at Central, and now watching the expressions on their faces as they put on their caps and gowns and ask the eternal question: Which side does the tassel go on?

Over the years, we have done some creative things to celebrate our EOP graduates. Initially, I had special ribbons in Central royal blue, with "EOP Graduate" spelled out in silver, to pin on their gowns. Back when the ceremony was held on the Central campus, I would reserve a room in the Student Center for a pre-graduation reception with cake, cookies, punch, and various graduation decorations. We'd invite students, parents, and staff, take pictures, and reminisce about the past before walking up the hill to the athletic field for the ceremony. I would be in the parking lot helping students line up by department and majors, with my camera ready to take individual and group pictures.

The outside ceremony was a fine event, always well attended. Then one year it rained buckets just as we were lining up, which led to a mad dash to the gym, the backup location. It was a chaotic mess (in every sense). People were soaked and there weren't enough seats to accommodate everyone. From that point on, graduation has been at the Hartford Civic Center (now the XL Center) in Hartford, which seats over 16,000 people. You can bring the whole family, and weather is not a factor.

I continued the tradition of being a marshal until a few years after I retired in 2009, and the last of "my" students had graduated. Because it represents the end of an era, I'll mention that the last graduation photo I took on campus was in 1986, of the 1982 EOP class, one of the best ever. I had the students meet in front of the administration building for a group shot that included Benjamin Torres, (EOP '71; there to receive his master's degree), Lillian Ortiz, Cynthia Lauria, Rosemary Anduaga (my wife's student in elementary school), Thair Gordon, Ginny Bermudez, Chau Tu La, and Clifford Scott. Program assistant Jimmy Knight and my wife Linda were receiving their sixth-year certificates, so it was a wonderful picture with the students, Jimmy, Linda, and me.

Unfortunately, one student was late and missed the picture: Aida Silva, a top student from the class of 1982. I remember one weekend, when we were going to take the group to Riverside Park for some recreation and downtime, Aida led a mini-revolution of students not wanting to go because of the tremendous workload. They wanted to spend the time completing their homework and papers. They lost that battle, and I made them go. Ultimately they had a good time, and it not only bonded the group but also made them more determined to be successful.

With the move to the civic center, as I was lining up students, I began gathering the EOP folks for a group shot before the processional began. I then took my place at the head of the processional to lead faculty into the main arena for the ceremony. After I helped organize the seating of students and faculty, my final assignment was to be at the stairway on the platform where the students, after going across the stage and shaking the president's hand, would come down the stairs to receive their diploma cases (the actual diploma came later). I helped the students off the stage, especially the women in heels, but my main motivation was to take pictures. I could hear the names being called and my camera was ready for the EOP kids—and later the athletes, when I became athletics director. During my time as director of EOP and athletics, I never missed a graduation ceremony and my prime spot to take pictures. I would get prints made and give each student their photo in a folder marked with the EOP logo and graduation symbol.

The CCSU graduation ceremony was held during Memorial Day weekend, on Friday when on the campus and on Saturday after it moved to the civic center. In the '70s and '80s I played on softball teams during the summers, and on Memorial Day weekend we would travel to Virginia to play in the world's largest softball tournament—108 teams competing over the weekend. Our team sponsor was the Little Casa Loma in Kensington, Connecticut. The owner, Belukar Magliochetti, was an elderly lady who loved her boys. We consumed a lot of pizza and beer during those days, but we brought back trophies, one year finishing sixth in a marathon of games. I would attend graduation, take pictures, then hop in the car and drive nine hours straight to Virginia, often arriving at 3 a.m. I'd get up around 8 a.m. for our first game at 9 a.m., and play softball all day Saturday on just a few hours of sleep.

When my softball playing days were over, in the mid-'80s, and graduation was at the civic center, I started a new Memorial Day tradition: camping with four or five other couples and their families. We had camping adventures with the Woodins, whose daughter, Sarah, I convinced to attend CCSU and who was a member of the band on our first NCAA basketball tournament trip; the Curetto family and Art Kittelson, close friends of the Woodins; and Karl Deutzmann, pastor of our church in Terryville, whose two sons attended Central.

We camped in Granville, Massachusetts, just north of the Connecticut border. Prospect Campground was about 65 miles from Hartford. I never missed graduation while camping. I would get up early and head to Hartford for the ceremony, then return to the campground later in the day. Sometimes I would bring back flowers from the stage decorations, but more often I brought balloons. At the end of the graduation ceremony, hundreds of blue and white balloons would be released from netting in the ceiling, signifying "Let the party begin!" Gathering up my camera and some balloons and/or plants, I drove back to the campground to join the others and continue the Memorial Day celebration, with a smile on my face from cheek to cheek because of what had just happened—another group of EOP students had graduated, helped by a summer experience that changed their lives and the lives of generations to follow.

Cultural Events Attended by EOP Students

Broadway and Off-Broadway Plays

- A Chorus Line
- Purlie
- Jelly's Last Jam
- The Wiz
- Once on This Island
- Dreamgirls
- 42nd Street
- Mama, I Want to Sing!
- Don't Bother Me, I Can't Cope
- Me and My Girl
- Five Guys Named Moe
- Starlight Express
- The Piano Lesson
- Two Trains Running

- The Tap Dance Kid
- For Colored Girls Who Have Considered Suicide / When the Rainbow Is Enuf
- Fences
- Annie
- Your Arms Too Short to Box with God
- Shakespeare (Stratford, CT)

Concerts

- The Jackson 5 at Madison Square Garden
- Newport Jazz Festival

Not Exactly Cultural, But Fun

- Riverside Park, Agawam, MA
- Great Adventure, Jackson, NJ

EOP
Athletes

A significant number of EOP students have distinguished themselves as athletes, with several achieving All-American status and a number selected for the Central Connecticut State University Hall of Fame.[3] With apologies in advance for anyone I leave out, here's a list of outstanding EOP athletes, beginning with members of the CCSU Hall of Fame:

Kevin Cranford, EOP 1976, Hall of Fame 2006. Kevin was All-American in track and field in the triple jump in 1981 and 1982. He still holds the CCSU record for the triple jump.

Adrienne Pitts, EOP 1979, Hall of Fame 1989. Adrienne was All-American in track and field. Outstanding in the classroom as well, she also served as an EOP counselor and, naturally, organized a field day for the summer program students.

Rich Leonard, EOP 1980, Hall of Fame 1992. Rich was All-American in basketball and is one of a handful of Blue Devils with over 1,000 points and 1,000 rebounds. He was

3 I am a member of the CCSU Hall of Fame, primarily for my success as athletics director from 1995–2009. I was also a basketball assistant and head coach, and as an undergraduate I played varsity baseball and basketball.

co-captain of a team ranked as high as sixth in the country in Division II, and made several trips to the NCAA tournament.

Hope Linthicum, EOP 1982, Hall of Fame 1993. Hope was All-American in basketball, was a magician with the ball, and is one of the top scorers in Central's basketball history.

Tajuana Sands, EOP 1983, Hall of Fame 2016. A teammate of Hope's, "T" was among the best rebounders in Central's history. Not that Hope missed a lot of shots, but when she did, "T" did her work on both the offensive and defensive boards.

Bryan Heron, EOP 1985, Hall of Fame 2000. Bryan was an outstanding basketball player who led the team in scoring and rebounding and ranks high on CCSU's all-time lists in both categories. His son, Mustapha, won three high school state championships in Connecticut and received a scholarship to Auburn University, where he led the team in scoring and rebounding as a freshman and was voted to the All-SEC second team after his recently completed sophomore season. He declared himself eligible for the NBA draft in April 2018.

Other Notable EOP Athletes

William "Billy" Wendt, EOP 1969, was a high-scoring guard and captain of the basketball team.

Doug McArthur, EOP 1969, was captain of the baseball team.

Gwen Bailey, EOP 1970, played basketball and later

became a coach. A serious injury caused her to need a wheelchair, but that hasn't stopped her.

Art Rodrigues, EOP 1974, was a sprinter and a distance runner on the track team.

Steve Naraine, EOP 1974, was a fierce linebacker on the football team.

John L. Williams, EOP 1975, was a member of the wrestling team and became an outstanding EOP counselor. He went on to become an engineer at Boeing, and I credit him with starting the EOP Scholarship Fund by sending the first check from a former student.

Chris White, EOP 1977, played forward for the basketball team. Despite being small for that position, he had tremendous spring in his legs and often out-rebounded much bigger players—and threw down some massive dunks.

Johnny Kidd, EOP 1980, one of the quickest basketball players ever to wear a Central uniform, was a three-year starter at point guard, with nearly 500 assists. Johnny is presently an assistant coach at Sacred Heart University. Fellow 1980 EOPer Rich Leonard became an All-American partly because of great passes from Johnny.

Wanda Sabbath, EOP 1980, played on the basketball team.

Tyrone Canino, EOP 1983, was a captain of the basketball team while I was coaching, and was in the top ten in rebounding in the country as a senior.

Sethe Thompson, EOP 1983, was a speedy point guard on the basketball team.

Scott Bosley, EOP 1984, played basketball and hit a game-winning shot during my head coaching tenure.

Montez Johnson, EOP 1987, was an outstanding offensive tackle and captain of the football team. Montez works at Central as an academic advisor and often counsels EOP students.

Ray McGhee, EOP 1988, was a two-sport athlete, in football and track, and also an EOP counselor. His son Raishaun graduated from Harvard in 2018, where he played defensive back on a team that won three Ivy League titles.

Cleon Francis, EOP 1988, played on the basketball team. He was an EOP counselor and is presently a director at ESPN.

Mark Ward, EOP 1988, was a shot putter for the track team.

Duane Sheriden, EOP 1990, played on the football team.

Robert Ford, EOP 1991, was a member of the boxing team, which began as a boxing club.

Ricardo Gibson, EOP 2006, was a defensive end on two conference championship football teams.

Several of the abovementioned athletes are being considered for CCSU Hall of Fame induction, and I anticipate that some will join their fellow EOP classmates there in the near future.

Other EOP-Style Programs in Connecticut

ConnCAP

Dr. Marco Kinsella

The Connecticut Collegiate Awareness and Preparation Program (ConnCAP) began in 1987 under the state's Board of Governors for Higher Education, with a mission to expand the number of students from disadvantaged environments who graduate from high school, and to prepare them with the necessary skills and motivation for success in college.

CCSU has been involved with ConnCAP from its inception. Due in part to our successful EOP program, we received a grant and had the largest ConnCAP program in the state, serving students from New Britain and Waterbury, two towns where EOP had successfully engaged with students for years. Thus, EOP was not only instrumental in CCSU acquiring the grant, but also helped ConnCAP recruit students because of strong ties already established in those cities.

ConnCAP provided services during the academic school year and the summer to supplement students' high school experience, starting in their freshman year. Students received course instruction in reading, writing, mathematics, science, and study skills; personal and career counseling; tutorial services; SAT preparation; college visitations and campus residential experiences; cultural enrichment activities; mentoring; community service programs; parental involvement activities; and college follow-up programs.

I am a mathematics teacher in a local high school and did my dissertation research on CCSU's ConnCAP. In the first eight years of the program, 400 students participated in ConnCAP at CCSU. One hundred sixty-eight had graduated from high school, while 194 were still enrolled in the program, an average retention rate of 84 percent.

In that same period, 137 ConnCAP students who had graduated enrolled in college for at least one semester. That represented an average college attendance rate for the program of 82 percent, compared to the national average of 55 percent. As I state in my dissertation, "The fact that the students completed the program, entered college, and completed a successful freshman year is a monument of sorts to the success of the ConnCAP program. Without the ConnCAP experience, many or most of these students would never have gone to college." And without the ConnCAP experience, many or most of the students who did go to college would not have survived their freshman year.

ConnCAP lost its funding in 2017. The program was quite successful for thirty years, increasing the number of college-eligible students from the inner cities of Connecticut. It was a great run and a successful one before budgetary issues, experienced throughout the state and country, eliminated the program. CCSU remains committed to the students presently in the program and will continue to provide some services, though limited to current students.

ConnCAP was a bridge to the EOP, a program funded by Central Connecticut State University for the last fifty years! Both programs helped ensure that young people entering the university would succeed. That is why it is so hard to believe that ConnCAP was terminated. As EOP celebrates its fiftieth anniversary in 2018, it's a shame that ConnCAP will not be alongside to celebrate.

In closing, I am fed up with politicians saying to educational institutions, "Do it for the kids. Work with less." Now I am asking them to back up their words and do it for the kids. It is hard to practice what the politicians preach. The time is now.

Larry Hall

It is with great respect and appreciation that I write this letter in support of university, state, and federal funding to support programs such as ConnCAP, Upward Bound, and EOP. I have been intimately involved with such programs since 1981, when I first entered Weaver High School.

I was selected to participate in the Upward Bound program at the University of Connecticut. In 1981 I met Mr. Robert Brown, who interviewed me at my home and told me the benefits of enrolling in such an outstanding program. I participated in the summer program for a few weeks and then needed to come home to be with my mother, who was battling cancer at the time. Though I never returned to the program, I saw the benefits and the impact it had on the lives of students who participated in the program.

Entering Central Connecticut State University in the fall of 1985, I became very familiar with the EOP program. Though I was not a participant, I quickly understood that my classmates had a connection entering the school that I did not. Kyle McDougald, one of my classmates from Weaver, participated in the program and as a result of our connection, I was able to meet many of the students who participated, and also came to know this legend named C. J.

Central was not a very diverse community at the time, and students who came through the program were able to bond and share in a common experience that bridged students from across the region in the vibrant summer academic, social, and cultural experience called EOP. They started Central with relationships. They started Central with mentors they could turn to in any situation. They started Central with a sense of pride and community. Many students from Connecticut's inner cities did not start their college careers with such benefits, unless they were enrolled in EOP. EOP was definitely "a summer that would change your life"!

As a result of my connection with members of the program and developing a relationship with the EOP office, I was afforded the opportunity to be hired as a counselor in the newly formed Connecticut Collegiate Awareness and Preparation Program (ConnCAP). During this period, I had a chance to work with first-generation/low-income students from New Britain and Waterbury. As counselors, we served two major roles: assisting teachers with classroom instruction and support, and assisting students with their social and behavioral skills. This experience changed my life. I saw working in higher education as an opportunity and a career.

My change of heart in making a change in my career choice led me to Sacred Heart University to work as a counselor in their newly formed Upward Bound Program, where I worked with low-income/first-generation students from the Bridgeport area. I worked with four different high schools at the time (three public and one private). I was beginning to understand even better the disparities in education and opportunity that exist within our state and across the country.

Students from all walks of life need exposure to higher education, and they need to be surrounded by mentors, teachers, and counselors who have their best interests at heart. At Sacred Heart, I was able to confirm this feeling and belief. I brought in Michael Ansarra, a friend/colleague and Cornell graduate, to speak to a group of students about college life. Little did I know that sitting there, listening keenly, was a young man named Ceasar Irby, who would later attend Cornell and subsequently become Dr. Ceasar Irby, a respected podiatric surgeon.

Leaving Upward Bound to return to Central and work in college admissions was exciting. However, that didn't compare to returning to Central as director of admissions, after being director of admissions at Western Connecticut State University. Life was coming full circle for me both personally and professionally. Central was home, and working with the EOP program was a great opportunity.

My first major event after returning was the EOP summer banquet. I make it a personal and professional opportunity to shake hands and congratulate young people each year on being able to successfully complete the summer program and enroll at Central for the upcoming fall semester. It may not mean much to the students but it means the world to me.

In this current climate, legislators and presidents at all levels seek to save money by cutting budgets or even eliminating funding for university, state, and federal programs. In my humble opinion, it is a mistake. Connecticut has the highest achievement gap in the nation. Connecticut is also one of the most diverse states in the country, with three of the poorest cities within its boundaries. This is not the time to eliminate funding. This is the time to add funding. In 2017, for the first time in its history, Harvard's incoming class had a majority of non-white students. Schools like Central continue to become more diverse by the year, not only in Connecticut but across the nation.

As I reflect upon my own personal journey, I have not known a time in my adult life that wasn't influenced by programs like ConnCAP and EOP. Not only have I worked in federal TRIO programs, but I have served on the board of directors for the Connecticut Talent Assistance Cooperative's Educational Opportunity Center for roughly fifteen years. These programs matter! They matter to students, families, high schools, and communities. Each student and generation should have a chance to succeed and compete within the global economy. These types of programs provide that legitimate avenue of enhanced support and opportunity for students. I endorse them wholeheartedly as an individual and as a professional. As we celebrate fifty years of the EOP, we celebrate a longstanding history of the contributions of these types of programs in general.

Tammy Grella

As a kid, my summers revolved around early mornings that faded into late nights filled with family and friends, baseball games, skinned knees, fighting with my older brother, and camping trips. For two glorious months the thoughts of school buses and mathematics were set aside and replaced with bicycles, ice cream, and coloring books.

I was thirteen in the summer of 1987, and suddenly my summers were about to change. I was given an opportunity to attend a new summer program that was just starting up at Central Connecticut State University. That program was ConnCAP.

While I had always been a decent student, and enjoyed school well enough, at thirteen I was not real thrilled at the prospect of "summer school." But my parents insisted, and off I went, backpack, pencils, and skepticism in tow.

Four summers later, in 1991, I stood proud as part of the first ever ConnCAP graduating class, feeling grateful not only for the many friends and wonderful memories I had gained, but more importantly for the confidence and sense of self that I had found. I went into my senior year as one of the top students in my class, eventually being inducted into the National Honor Society. With a strong academic résumé and fairly good athletic ability, I knew that college was in my future! After applying and being accepted to four schools, I chose to attend the university that helped me gain the skills I needed to become a better student, and the work ethic that would help me throughout my life. In the fall of 1992, I enrolled as a freshman at CCSU.

ConnCAP never felt like a summer school. Yes, there were classes . . . and work . . . but there were friends and there was laughter. There were educational trips and trips that were just plain fun. ConnCAP provided an opportunity to discover and develop yourself as a student. For me, it helped create the possibility of a successful future.

After college I became a teacher, and while I might not remember the actual content of what we learned way back when in those summer classrooms, what I do recall is that our teachers had supplied an atmosphere where it was safe: safe to fail and to succeed; safe to take a risk and to create; safe to be proud and to ask for help. These are the values that I learned by being a part of the ConnCAP program, and they are the values I try to bring into my classroom today, almost thirty years later.

I received my bachelor's degree in Fine Arts in theatre design from CCSU in spring of 1996, and that fall I began teaching theatre at the Forman School in Litchfield, Connecticut. This past September, I started my twenty-second year there. Forman is a private, college-prep boarding school for students who have a diagnosed learning disability. While the vast majority of those students come from families with money, they also come damaged from years of being told they are lazy and dumb because they just can't keep up with their classmates. Their college futures are uncertain, and sometimes, unlikely. They feel defeated and distrustful of teachers and education in general. Much of the work we do in the classroom is similar to the work that was done with us at ConnCAP: teaching confidence and self-advocacy; teaching young people to stand as independent learners.

This past year, I had the opportunity to return to CCSU and participate in a couple of theatre courses. I was excited about returning to a college campus, and I knew that it was time for me to update some of my classroom lessons. I shared this experience with my Forman students, and they often knew when I had a presentation due or was working on a writing assignment. I felt it was important for them to know that learning never ends, that it's a lifelong pursuit, and that teachers are also students.

By their senior year, most of our students are successfully accepted into a wide range of colleges, and their futures are far different than they were upon arrival. This is not so different than the experience that hundreds of students have gotten through the ConnCAP program.

ConnCAP is an immensely important program, at a very critical time in a young person's life when there can be confusion and self-doubt. My life was touched by being involved in the ConnCAP program. It helped me to focus on the positive things that can come from school and gave me the desire to continue my education—as well as the confidence to know that I could. I am extremely grateful.

Jermaine Evans

Back in eighth grade I saw an opportunity to get out of class early to attend a meeting about ConnCAP. I did not take it seriously at first. In fact, I felt a certain resentment toward the program because I was spending five weeks of the summer going to class instead of getting a summer job like the rest of my friends. It wasn't until my senior year in high school that I came to realize how much of an effect ConnCAP had on me. I was exposed to things that an inner-city kid would never dream of seeing, such as Broadway plays and college recruitment fairs. This experience helped to shape my academic career and enabled me to graduate fourth in my class. That is owed all to ConnCAP.

Not enough can be said about the dedication the staff showed us each summer. They wanted all of us to succeed not just in school, but in life. It is a shame that the program is ending. This program is needed more than ever in today's climate. I can honestly say I don't know where I would be in life without the support system and values that the people involved with ConnCAP instilled in me.

I remember years ago, when C. J. said that as a condition of putting me on one of the ConnCAP brochures I had to do him proud and live up to the responsibility of representing the program in that fashion. That made me strive to be a success story for ConnCAP. I attended Central Connecticut State University, earning a bachelor's degree in Mass Media Communications (1997), and got a job upon graduation at Fox 61 television. Two years later I decided to pursue my master's degree in Educational Media, also at Central Connecticut State University (2001). Presently I am a senior coordinator in Production Operations at ESPN.

Thanks for your help!

Eastern Connecticut State University's STEP/CAP

Now in its thirty-fourth consecutive year, the Summer Transition at Eastern Program/Contract Admissions Program (STEP/CAP) continues to thrive. At present, more than 250 students who have participated in STEP/CAP are enrolled on a full-time basis. Year after year, conditionally admitted STEP/CAP students are retained and graduate at rates that are comparable to students who were traditionally admitted to Eastern. Since 2000, STEP/CAP six-year graduation rates have more than doubled, while four-year graduation rates have tripled.

By coming to STEP/CAP and agreeing to its six-week residential summer experience, students work on college-level courses that award a minimum of three and a maximum of seven credits that can count toward graduation. Successful completion of the program affords students the opportunity to begin their freshman year with 10 to 20 percent of the thirty credits completed. In many ways, STEP/CAP becomes a step ahead. In recent years, STEP/CAP has averaged cohorts of sixty to sixty-five students.

In 1980, under TRIO federal funding, the Contract Admissions Program (CAP) began. Housed in the university's Division of Academic Affairs, it was a special admissions program that provided intensive freshman year support, including mentoring, tutoring, counseling, and other activities. STEP/CAP enhanced this program by also requiring STEP, a rigorous academic pre-college summer bridge program.

STEP/CAP began in 1983 under the direction of Floyd Bagwell, assisted by Margaret Hébert. For over a decade, the program operated under TRIO federal grant funds, then for the next two decades under grants from the Connecticut Office of Higher Education. Eastern has always matched these funds, and Eastern currently provides full funding for the program.

STEP/CAP alumni are teachers, authors, counselors, administrators, social workers, entrepreneurs, managers, and mentors. They have published; they have pursued careers in business, education, public health, government, security, journalism, broadcasting, and more. Many have completed master's degrees, several have completed doctoral degrees, and at least one is an MD.

Following Mr. Bagwell's retirement in 2007, Dr. Hébert served as the program director until her retirement in 2012. Currently the program is directed by Dr. Fredrick Hornung.

Southern Connecticut State University's SEOP

Southern Connecticut State University is an intentionally diverse learning community that is committed to academic excellence, access, social justice, and service for the public good. As a part of its mission, Southern is committed to providing postsecondary educational opportunities to students who show promise for success, but have faced educational or economic disadvantages that have impacted their preparedness for college.

In 1972 the Southern Educational Opportunity Program (SEOP) was created, with the belief that students' success is ultimately determined by their motivation, regardless of personal circumstances, and that they can graduate with the assistance of a caring, supportive community of educators.

Hundreds of students who participated in SEOP in the last four decades have successfully graduated from Southern and have been positive contributors to their local, state, national, and international communities.

The program consists of the following components:

- Summer Academy
- Academic-Year Success Initiatives

SEOP helps students:

- Make a successful transition to Southern
- Develop a strong foundation for continuous success during their first year
- Attain continuous academic and personal success through graduation

- Graduate from the university prepared for career and/ or graduate / professional academic success

Wesleyan University

Miguel Peralta, Director, Pre-College Access Programs and Upward Bound Math-Science

Wesleyan University has had a rich history of supporting low-income, first-generation, and underrepresented students, having hosted a TRIO program on campus for over fifty years.

In 1966, Wesleyan was awarded a federal grant to serve the Middletown community through an Upward Bound program. This was the result of the hard work of a group of community leaders that included Peter Budryk, Upward Bound's first project director. With Peter strategically leading the charge, Wesleyan's Upward Bound program was essential in building the community of EOP programs throughout the state, while helping its participants realize their dreams of a college education.

Peter's leadership in the state EOP community led to the establishment of the Connecticut Collegiate Awareness and Preparation Program (ConnCAP) in 1987, under Connecticut's Board of Governors for Higher Education. As a result, the Wesleyan Upward Bound program was joined by a ConnCAP program to increase the services and number of schools that the burgeoning department could serve. Eventually the Upward Bound and ConnCAP programs successfully served hundreds of students from Middletown and the surrounding towns of Portland and Meriden. The US Department of Education, in national competitions in 1986 and 1996, selected the Wesleyan

University Upward Bound program as a National Model Program.

Another noteworthy achievement of the Wesleyan Upward Bound program was Peter's creation of the Great Hollow Wilderness School (GHWS) in 1969. The GHWS essentially combined Upward Bound with the Outward Bound wilderness experience program, allowing disadvantaged youth to experience new things and unlock the true potential Peter knew existed within them. When seniors were asked at the senior dinner about their most memorable and impactful experiences as an Upward Bound student, students would immediately say their Great Hollow Wilderness School experience.

Although the Upward Bound program was defunded after forty-five successful years, the spirit of TRIO is still alive at the university through Upward Bound Math-Science (UBMS) and the Ronald E. McNair Post-Baccalaureate programs. Inspired by the original Upward Bound program, UBMS serves students from Middletown, Meriden, and New Britain. The McNair program aids Wesleyan undergraduate students in their quest for postgraduate degrees.

We congratulate CCSU's Educational Opportunity Program on celebrating its fiftieth year serving disadvantaged youths throughout their college careers!

A Summary of Academic Research on EOP-Style Programs

By Robert Jost

In "Rethinking College Readiness," (2008), author David T. Conley observes that first-generation students who struggle to become successful in college, especially during their first year, often fail and become alienated, which results in them dropping out. Based on this finding, Conley concludes that first-generation students who can interact with their peers and faculty members, have knowledge of how the system works, and can take advantage of support services offered will meet with success in college and persist. EOP programs are structured to provide the resources students need to meet the criteria for success that Conley has outlined.

Self-Efficacy

Albert Bandura defines self-efficacy as "one's beliefs in one's capabilities to mobilize the motivation, cognitive resources, and courses of action needed to exercise control over task demands." (Bandura, 1990, p. 316). Bandura first introduced the construct in 1977 as part of his theory of social learning, which posits that individuals are constantly learning by means of communication, observation, and interaction with others through social mechanisms that do not require direct reinforcement, a concept referred to as vicarious learning (Ward, 2003). He asserted that "people's level of motivation, affective states, and actions are based more on what they believe than on what is objectively true" (Bandura, 1997, p. 2).

The four sources of information that contribute to an individual's self-efficacy have been identified as mastery experiences, observational or vicarious experiences, social persuasions, and psychological feedback (Bandura, 1997). He noted further that of the four information sources, mastery experiences played the largest role. Since Bandura introduced the theory of self-efficacy in 1977, research has been conducted in areas as diverse as medicine, sports, business, and careers to determine the impact the construct has on individuals and their achievement levels. In the area of education, studies to determine the role self-efficacy plays in students' achievement and persistence to complete tasks are being conducted, seeking ways teachers can engage students and assist them in reaching their potential.

Schunk developed a model to describe the "reciprocal influence between self-efficacy, task engagement variables and achievement behaviors" (1987, p. 179). He described his model using the example of a student learning a new educational concept. Students arrive with different beliefs concerning whether they will be successful based on their prior experiences. Once engaged in the learning process, they are influenced by social and institutional variables. As the process evolves, students receive cues as to how they are performing the required tasks. The cues the students receive are based on the four sources of information that Bandura believes contribute to self-efficacy. The students use the information they obtain to ascertain their efficacy for future educational activities.

Recognizing the positive role self-efficacy can play in influencing a student to believe they can undertake a difficult task and persist to achieve a goal, researchers have undertaken studies with specific student populations. Studies conducted by Multon, Brown, and Lent (1991), and Pajares and Miller (1994), concluded that self-efficacy has a positive impact on students' achievement and retention. Zimmerman, Bandura, and Martinez-Pons (1992) found there was a link between a student's sense of self-efficacy and the goals they set for themselves academically. The higher the student's sense of self efficacy, the more difficult goals they set.

Zimmerman states that "self-efficacy is assumed to be responsive to changes in personal context and outcomes, whether experienced directly, vicariously, verbally, or physiologically," and as a result, "self-efficacy beliefs are studied as indicators of change during instructional interventions" (2000, p. 88). Numerous studies to date have established the positive outcomes educational interventions can have on students' self-efficacy, and how a heightened sense of self-efficacy can impact a student's academic achievement and persistence.

Solberg and Villarreal conducted a study to determine the impact of self-efficacy on the personal adjustment of Hispanic students to college. The researchers were aware that the transition from high school to college can be stressful for students, and wanted to examine if self-efficacy beliefs eased this transition for Hispanic students, who are considered members of an underrepresented group. Their findings supported the hypothesis that self-efficacy expectations would have a positive impact on distress ratings for Hispanic students. This led the researchers to conclude that a high level of self-efficacy could not only positively help students deal with the stress of college, but also it could also influence their persistence (Solberg and Villarreal, 1997).

Research by Schreiner et al. highlights the fact that students who have positive interactions with faculty and staff both inside and outside of the classroom develop a sense of confidence that the university cares about them. Drawing on previous research by Bean and Eaton (2002), the researchers concluded that this "in turn bolsters the students' sense of self-efficacy that they can survive and even thrive in the organization" (2011, p. 323). Research by Braxton et al. (2004) concluded that as a result of heightened self-efficacy, students are more likely to become socially integrated into the campus community, and this social integration can positively equate to persistence. This is noteworthy since Pike and Kuh (2005) found that first-generation students, when compared to their non-first-generation counterparts, were less likely to be academically and socially engaged on campus, and that this contributed to their not persisting.

Unfortunately, access to college and assistance to complete a college degree is still not a reality for many first-generation, low-income students from underrepresented groups. With the rising cost of tuition, they often cannot afford higher education, even with assistance. Research by Kuh et al. (2007) highlights the fact that the ability of students to attend college is influenced by the availability of financial aid. In addition, with more students from low-income families entering college there has been "a decline in the average level of academic preparedness" (Baum et al., 2013, p. 20).

A main component of the federal Higher Education Act is Title 4 (the Student Assistance Act), which established Student Support Services (SSS) and other efforts, such as the EOP bridge programs. Both acts provide first-generation students with special assistance to gain admission to colleges, and to have the tools they need to ensure their persistence and success. Researchers McKenna and Lewis (1986) note that it is imperative that first-generation students be introduced to college on a multitude of levels, socially, academically, culturally, and emotionally. Research has proven that students who participate in EOP face a smoother transition from high school to college and have better persistence rates (Ackerman, 1991; Garcia, 1991; Walpole et al., 2008).

As institutions strive to retain students, it is imperative that they develop and implement strategies that will assist in achieving this goal. Pascarella and Terenzini found that "a significant portion of student attrition might be prevented through timely and carefully planned institutional interventions" (1980, p. 61). Educational opportunity programs are one effective intervention. These EOPs not only bridge the summer between high school graduation and the start of freshman year of college, but also continue to provide services for students from the start of their college career until graduation day. Research has proven that summer bridge programs are a positive factor in college retention (Ackerman, 1991; Garcia, 1991; Robert and Thomason, 1994; Santa Rita and Bacote, 1996). In addition, research highlights the fact that students who participate in EOPs have shown higher persistence and degree attainment than their peers who did not participate in the programs (US Department of Education, 2005).

An EOP provides first-generation students with a vehicle to build social and cultural capital, referring to an individual's social networks and acquaintances (Stolle-McAllister, 2011). Students from low-income families are often disadvantaged since their socioeconomic environment does not provide them with the tools necessary to succeed in school, such as a supportive family, academic support, and successful role models (Cabera et al., 2006). By failing to teach students the importance of cultural capital, schools not only "reproduce existing inequalities but make it difficult to break the circle in which cultural capital is added to cultural capital" (1977; as cited in Cabera et al., 2006, p. 83).

According to Portes (1998), social capital is the knowledge gained from, and the access provided by, an individual's social network. This is noteworthy since first-generation students often only know acquaintances from their homogenous background. Therefore, it would be difficult for them to build social capital unless they ventured outside their own milieu. N. Lin (2000) notes that since these students are only exposed to students of similar backgrounds, this can cause their social capital to be reduced. Dryfoos (1990) concludes that students could be considered as high risk for failing in school based on their peer group and the quality of the neighborhood in which they reside. Research concludes that the majority of first-generation students are hampered by the fact that they "struggle to navigate the middle-class culture of higher education, learn the 'rules of the game,' and take advantage of college resources" (Stephens, Hamedani, and Destin, 2014, p. 944).

The influence of cultural capital was examined in a 2007 study dealing with mastery of the "role of college student" by traditional and first-generation college students. Specific emphasis was placed on how the students viewed the expectations of faculty members. The results indicated that the cultural capital traditional students had obtained from their families and other resources allowed them to have a much deeper understanding of what the faculty member expected from them. They concluded that traditional students' use of the cultural capital they had acquired over the years gave them an advantage in being successful and persisting. They noted that this supports Bourdieu's theory of reproduction "where those that come from an advantaged background maintain that advantage into the next generation" (Collier and Morgan, 2007, p. 442).

Bandura argues that individuals are products of their social networks. A vital component of EOP is the fact that they provide students the opportunity to build a strong sense of self-efficacy. This goal is achieved through the use of mentors and peer mentors, who offer continuous support and encouragement and show the students that they can indeed succeed and have a chance in college. The peer mentors also convey valuable "college knowledge," which according to Roderick et al. (2009) provides first-generation students with an understanding of acceptable college norms and culture. First-generation students who form relationships with other first-generation students allow themselves "to feel as if they are staying true to their own sense of self" (Cushman, 2007; as cited in Woosley and Shepler, 2011, p. 703). Cushman's study "indicated that first generation students may feel their fellow college students often seem to be members of a club of insiders." Cushman's research highlights the myriad of conflicting emotions that first-generation students need to deal with, along with the stress that naturally accompanies students' transition to college. This situation only adds to the issues impacting their success and makes their integration into the campus community more difficult.

Milem and Berger (1997) highlighted the results of research conducted by Davis (1991), and Taylor and Howard-Hamilton (1995), which provides evidence that African-American students who were involved in campus activities had a lower dropout rate. Also, African-American students who were enrolled in predominately white institutions, where they were actively involved in campus activities such as clubs, community service, and sports, were more likely "to develop a positive racial identity" (Miliem and Berger, 1997, p. 644). The research of Taylor and Howard-Hamilton emphasized the positive correlation between campus involvement and retention of African-American students at institutions where they are considered members of an underrepresented group.

As institutions strive to retain students, it is imperative that they develop and implement strategies that assist in achieving this goal. Educational opportunity programs are an intervention that is gaining in popularity. The programs not only bridge the summer between high school graduation and the start of the freshman year of college, but continue to provide services for students until graduation day. Research has proven that SSS/EOP programs are a positive factor in college retention (Ackerman, 1991; Garcia, 1991; Robert and Thomason, 1994; Santa Rita and Bacote, 1996).

Kallison and Stadler note that EOPs provide students with "academic instruction, tutoring, study skills instruction, and mentoring/counseling/advising" (2012, p. 343). A cornerstone of EOP is the academic component, which provides students assistance in reading and writing on the college level. In a summary of the best practices to employ in college teaching, Drummond cited the value of mentorship, academic counseling, and individual tutoring, all of which are components of EOPs (1995; as cited in Michael et al., 2010).

Today, lawmakers seeking to curb what many believe is out of control spending on education have targeted remedial education as an unnecessary drain on state budgets. McCurrie (2009) cites the Spellings Commission Report, released in 2006 and named after then US Secretary of Education Margaret Spellings, which has raised questions about the effectiveness of summer bridge programs, the cornerstone of the majority of EOPs. At the same time, the report criticizes colleges and universities for their failure to recruit and retain first-generation students, the population that EOPs serve. In light of this criticism, and since federal and state funding is essential to EOPs, college administrators are anxious to show the value of EOPs. Conley defines college readiness as "the level of preparation a student needs in order to enroll and succeed without remediation—in a credit-bearing general education course at a post-secondary institution" (2008, p. 24). Research has shown that students who enter college underprepared to meet the expectations of college courses have a negative impact on graduation rates.

Educational opportunity programs provide students with academic and social skills that they need to succeed in college prior to the start of their freshman year, then offer support to participants as they progress through college. The goal is to promote college access, retention, and completion rates for low-income, first-generation students from underrepresented groups (Garcia & Paz, 2009). The majority of programs adhere to the philosophy of Tinto (1997), that by ensuring a supportive and motivating environment for first-generation students these students will achieve "academic and social integration." Drummond states that "student engagement and a student's sense of personal responsibility are significant factors in academic success" (1995; as cited in Michael et al., 2010, p. 971). Engstrom and Tinto (2008) note that providing access without support is not providing real opportunity for first-generation students.

Studies have highlighted the psychological benefits first-generation students garner from seeing students who come from backgrounds similar to theirs enter college and succeed (Oyserman and Destin, 2010; Stephens et al., 2012). Hu (2010) conducted a study to determine the relationship between student engagement in social activities and their persistence in college. A major finding was that students who had high levels of engagement in social activities were likely to persist and complete a degree program. When academic engagement was factored in with social engagement, it is noteworthy that the group of students who exhibited low-middle academic engagement along with high social engagement had the highest rate of persistence at 97.1 percent (Hu, 2010, p. 101). This finding reinforces the theory that for students to meet with success, they need to be both academically and socially integrated into the campus community. This belief also impacts the students' self-efficacy beliefs by providing positive mentors and models.

One major component of EOPs is peer mentoring. Bean states, "Few would deny that the social lives of students in college and their exchanges with others inside and outside the institution are important in retention decisions" (2005; p. 227).

One way to integrate students into the campus community is through peer mentoring, an integral component of EOPs. Johnson noted that "mentoring was first studied in higher education in 1911 at the University of Michigan by faculty in the engineering department; however, it was not until 1988 that an attempt was made to identify roles and functions of mentoring in the education literature" (as cited in Crisp and Cruz, 2009, p. 535). Today, institutions of higher education are faced with the dual dilemma of shrinking monetary resources coupled with increased pressure to retain students, and therefore increase graduation rates. The concept of peer mentoring is a method that institutions can employ to provide a valuable service to their students at a relatively low cost, while at the same time achieving their goals of increasing student retention rates and persistence.

Shojai et al. (2014) believe that mentoring relationships described as developmental, where human interaction is reciprocal, can be an integral component in programs designed to improve the academic performance of college students who have been identified as at risk. They base their theory on the premise that after conducting t-tests, they found an increase in the GPA of student mentees post-mentoring for at least three semesters during which time no other interventions took place. Research by Cushman highlights the fact that first-generation students who are able to establish and maintain mentoring relationships with peers who are also first-generation students "feel as if they are staying true to their own sense of self" (2007; as cited in Woosley and Shepler, 2011, p. 703). Furthermore, if these students are also able to establish mentoring relationships with faculty members, research has shown they are likely to persist after their first year.

Peer mentoring that addresses academic and social integration of students hopefully will be an intervention that has a positive impact on reducing attrition. Pascarella and Terenzini (1980) postulate that institutions are in a position to address and prevent attrition by instituting well-planned and timely interventions, and the peer mentoring component of EOPs meets this criterion.

In a peer mentor relationship, the mentor is the mentee's equal and therefore has no formal authority over them. However, it is expected that the mentor will have more experience and a certain level of achievement in the environment in which the mentoring takes place. Jacobi (1991) describes the mentor/mentee relationship as a reciprocal one, where both receive benefits from the relationship. This is similar to the reciprocal relationship Bandura describes in his theory: The relationship takes place in a social context and involves modeling and observing behaviors. Jacobi outlines specific functions of the mentor, one or all of which may be present in the relationship. These functions apply to university staff, faculty, and peers, all of whom serve as mentors in the program. A mentor provides "emotional and psychological support, direct assistance with career and professional development and role modeling" (Jacobi, 1991, p. 513). Eighteen years later Crisp and Cruz updated Jacobi's 1991 research and concluded that the three components identified as being the foundation of mentoring were still supported by the literature. They noted "findings indicated a positive relationship or an impact of mentoring on student persistence and/or grade point average of undergraduate students" (Crisp and Cruz, 2009, p. 532).

Peer mentoring differs from traditional mentoring. Because

the mentor and mentee are close in age, they often develop a relationship since the mentor can use their own experiences to relate to the mentee, and often they are more empathetic to the situation the mentee is experiencing (Angelique et al., 2002). Coleman, McDill, and Rigsby note that a considerable amount of research on the pre-collegiate level has shown that students are influenced by their peer groups, and that this influence can be used to "enhance student involvement in the learning process" (as cited in Astin, 1984, p. 528). Most peer mentoring programs focus on two areas, which include "providing advice, support, and information related to course work, task accomplishment, study skills, or a psychosocial function (providing emotional and psychological support)" (Kram and Isbella, as cited in Terrion and Leonard, 2010, p. 85).

The aim of the peer mentoring relationship is to pair first-generation students needing assistance in academic courses or with social issues related to adjusting to the college environment with first-generation students who are more experienced upper-class students (Terrion and Leonard, 2010). Persistence and completion rates are two measures that universities use to determine if they are successfully meeting the needs of their students. Lang and Ford identified the following factors that have an effect on student success:

1. The inability to meet university academic standards

2. the inability to adapt to a new social and academic environment

3. changes in personal goals and aspirations

4. lack of motivation and clearly defined goals

5. priority of other commitments such as work, family, or financial difficulty

6. incongruence between an institution's orientation and approach desired by the individual (as cited by Salinitri, 2005, p. 854)

The factors Lang and Ford identified fit the profile of a first-generation student. Based on this information, Salinitri developed a pilot peer mentoring program to assist low-achieving, first-year students in coping with issues that could have a negative impact on their college experience. The results of the study indicated that mentors had an overwhelmingly positive effect on assisting their mentees in identifying and accessing resources that were available at the university. Having experienced what the mentees were going through, the peer mentors provided invaluable advice and guidance in setting up schedules, time management skills, and study habits. Additionally, the mentees reported that by having mentors who shared their personal experiences with them, they had a positive role model (Salinitri, 2005). Based on Jacobi's criteria for what areas a successful mentor should address, this group of mentors definitely provided their mentees with a valuable experience.

Sanchez, Bauer, and Paronto conducted a study over a four-year period that addressed the effect of peer mentoring, which they viewed as a positive intervention on the attitudes and behaviors of students. They also studied the way in which peer mentoring eventually impacted issues that were pertinent to the higher education setting, but that had not been fully explored before their study. The study focused on a mentoring model that was based on "an established theory of human behavior and present information on the attitudinal and behavioral effects of a formal peer mentoring program of university students in a large Midwestern school of business" (Sanchez et al., 2006, p. 25). Researchers state that "peer mentoring programs hold the potential to increase student involvement for both mentors and protégés". The results of the study indicated that the low-cost peer mentoring program had a positive effect on both students' retention and persistence. Students reported a high rate of overall satisfaction with their experience at the university. The study concluded that peer mentoring programs did indeed have a positive impact on student retention rates, while at the same time offering university administrators an inexpensive way to achieve goals set by the institution. It was the hope of the researchers that their study would provide valuable information to administrators seeking a low-cost program that had a positive effect on student retention and persistence.

In addition to providing a successful retention strategy, peer mentoring programs provide a number of benefits to all the participants. Research conducted by Pope has shown "those students who are involved in mentoring programs are more fulfilled by their experiences in college than individuals who are not involved in these programs" (Budge, 2006, p. 78). The training peer mentors receive is essential to their overall experience and assists them in building valuable skills for dealing with various situations that might occur. Peer mentors often noted that they relied on previous peer mentors as role models to determine which tactics worked and which ones did not (Benjamin, 2007).

The STEP/CAP program at ECSU is structured to meet all the needs of students, both academic and social. Participants lamented that at times when they are stressed or overwhelmed with school work, they wish they could return to the six weeks in the summer when their small group thought everything was possible. I believe the program highlights what Thayer (2000) pointed out, which was that strategies to retain and assist first-generation students are readily transferable to the general student population. With institutions dealing with issues of retention and persistence, they should borrow policies that EOP, STEP/CAP, and similar programs have implemented to assist students.

I would be remiss if I did not point out that a significant reason for the success of the STEP/CAP program over the last thirty-seven years has been the three dedicated individuals who served as the director. They all had a passion for helping first-generation students achieve their potential, and from talking to students and reviewing archival materials it was evident they succeeded. The students were eternally grateful that someone cared enough to help them and more importantly saw their potential and believed in them.

References

Ackermann, S. P. (1991). The benefits of summer bridge programs for underrepresented and low-income students. *College and University, 66*(4), 201-208.

Angelique, H., Kyle, K., & Taylor, E. (2002). Mentors and Muses: New Strategies for Academic Success. *Innovative Higher Education, 26*(3), 195-209. http://dx.doi.org/ 10.1023/A:1017968906264

Astin, A. (1984). Student involvement: A Developmental Theory for Higher Education. *Journal of College Student Personnel, 25,* 297-308.

Bandura, A. (1977). *Social Learning Theory*. Englewood Cliffs, NJ: Prentice Hall.

Bandura, A. (1986). *Social Foundations of Thought and Action: A Social Cognitive Theory*. Englewood Cliffs, NJ: Prentice Hall.

Bandura, A. (1993). Perceived Self-Efficacy in Cognitive Development and Functioning. *Educational Psychologist, 28*(2), 117-148. http://dx.doi.org/10.1207/s15326985ep2802_3

Bandura, A. (1996). *Self-Efficacy: The Exercise of Control*. New York, NY: Freeman.

Bandura, A., & Others, A. (1996). Multifaceted Impact of Self-Efficacy Beliefs on Academic Functioning. *Child Development, 67*(3), 1206-22.

Baum, S., Kurose, C., & McPherson, M. S. (2013). An Overview of American Higher Education. *The Future of Children, 23*(1), 17-39.

Bean, J., & Eaton, S. B. (2002). The Psychology Underlying Successful Retention Practices. *Journal of College Student Retention: Research, Theory, & Practice, 3*(1), 73-89.

Bean, J. P. (2005). Nine Themes of College Student Retention. In A. Seidman (Ed.), College student retention (pp. 215-243). Westport, MA: Praeger Publishers.

Benjamin, M. (2007). Role Construction of Residential Learning Community Peer Mentors. *Journal of College and University Student Housing, 34*(2), 31 42.

Budge, S. (2006). Peer Mentoring in Post-Secondary Education: Implications for Research and Practice. *Journal of College Reading and Learning, 37*(1), 73-87.

Cabrera, A. F., Deil-Amen, R., Prabhu, R., Terenzini, P. T., Lee, C., & Franklin, R. E., Jr. (2006). Increasing the College Preparedness of At-Risk Students. *Journal of Latinos & Education, 5*(2), 79-97. http://dx.doi.org/10.1207/s1532771xjle0502_2

Conley, D. T. (2008). Rethinking college readiness. *New Directions for Higher Education, 2008*(144), 3-13. http://dx.doi.org/10.1002/he.321

Crisp, G., & Cruz, I. (2009). Mentoring College Students: A Critical Review of the Literature Between 1990 and 2007. *Research in Higher Education, 50*(6), 525-545. http://dx.doi.org/10.1007/s11162-009-9130-2

Dryfoos, J. D. (1990) *Adolescents at Risk: Prevalence and Prevention.* New York, NY: Oxford University Press.

Engstrom, C., & Tinto, V. (2008). Access Without Support Is Not Opportunity. *Change, 40*(1), 46.

Garcia, P. (1991). Summer Bridge: Improving Retention Rates for Underprepared Students. *Journal of the Freshman Year Experience, 3*(2), 91-105.

Garcia, L. D., & Paz, C. C. (2009). Evaluation of Summer Bridge Programs. *About Campus, 14*(4), 30-32.

Hu, S. (2011). Reconsidering the Relationship Between Student Engagement and Persistence in College. *Innovative Higher Education, 36*(2), 97-106.

Jacobi, M. (1991). Mentoring and Undergraduate Academic Success: A Literature Review. *Review of Educational Research, 61*(4), 505-532.

Kallison, J. M., Jr., & Stader, D. L. (2012). Effectiveness of Summer Bridge Programs in Enhancing College Readiness. *Community College Journal of Research and Practice, 5*, 340-357. http://dx.doi.org/10.1080/10668920802708595

Kuh, G. D., Kinzie, J., Buckley, J. A., Bridges, B. K., & Hayek, J. C. (2007). Piecing together the student success puzzle: Research, propositions, and recommendations. *ASHE Higher Education Report, 32*(5), 1-182. http://dx.doi.org/10.1002/aehe.3205

Kuh, G. D., & Kinzie, J. (2005). *Student Success in College: Creating Conditions That Matter* (1st ed.). San Francisco, CA: Jossey-Bass.

Lin, N. (2000). Inequality in Social Capital. *Contemporary Sociology, 29*(6), 785-795.

McCurrie, M. (2009). Measuring Success in Summer Bridge Programs: Retention Efforts and Basic Writing. *Journal of Basic Writing, 28*(2), 28-49.

Michael, A. E., Dickson, J., Ryan, B., & Koefer, A. (2010). College Prep Blueprint for Bridging and Scaffolding Incoming Freshmen: Practices That Work. *College Student Journal, 44*(4), 969.

Milem, J. F., & Berger, J. B. (1997). A Modified Model of College Student Persistence: Exploring the Relationship Between Astin's Theory of Involvement and Tinto's Theory of Student Departure. *Journal of College Student Development, 38*(4), 387-400.

Multon, K. D., Brown, S. D., & Lent, R. W. (1991). Relation of self-efficacy beliefs to academic outcomes: A meta-analytic investigation. *Journal of Counseling Psychology, 38*, 30-38.

Oyserman, D., & Destin, M. (2010). Identity-Based Motivation: Implications for Intervention. *Counseling Psychologist, 38*(7), 1001-1043. http://dx.doi.org/10.1177/ 0011000010374775

Pajares, F., & Miller, M. D. (1994). Role of Self-Efficacy and Self-Concept Beliefs in Mathematical Problem Solving: A Path Analysis. *Journal of Educational Psychology, 86*(2), 193-203.

Pascarella, E. T., & Terenzini, P. T. (1980). Predicting Freshman Persistence and Voluntary Dropout Decisions from a Theoretical Model. *The Journal of Higher Education, 51*(1), 60-75. http://dx.doi.org/10.2307/1981125

Portes, A. (1998). *Social capital: Its origins and applications in modern sociology.* http://dx. doi.org/10.1146/annurev.soc.24.1.1

Robert, E., & Thomson, G. (1994). Learning Assistance and the Success of Underrepresented Students at Berkeley. *Journal of Developmental Education, 17*(3), 4-14.

Roderick, M. R., Nagaoka, J. K., & Coca, V. (2009). College Readiness for All: The Challenge for Urban High Schools. *The Future of Children, 19*(1), 185-210.

Salinitri, G. (2005). The Effects of Formal Mentoring on the Retention Rates for First-Year, Low Achieving Students. *Canadian Journal of Education, 28*(4), 853-873.

Sanchez, R. J., Bauer, T. N., & Paronto, M. E. (2006). Peer-Mentoring Freshmen: Implications for Satisfaction, Commitment and Retention to Graduation. *Academy of Management Learning & Education, 5*(1), 25-37. http://dx.doi.org/10.5465/AMLE.2006.20388382

Santa Rita, Emilio, & Bacote, Joseph B. (1996). *The Benefits of College Discovery Prefreshman Summer Program for Minority and Low Income Students.* 1996.

Schreiner, L. A., Noel, P., Anderson, E., & Cantwell, L. (2011). The Impact of Faculty and Staff on High-Risk College Student Persistence. *Journal of College Student Development, 52*(3), 321-338.

Schunk, D. H. (1989). Self-Efficacy and Achievement Behaviors. *Educational Psychology Review, 1*, 173-208.

Shojai, S., Davis, W., & Root, P. (2014). Developmental Relationship Programs: An Empirical Study of the Impact of Peer-Mentoring Programs. *Contemporary Issues in Education Research (Online), 7*(1), 31.

Solberg, V. S., & Villarreal, P. (1997). Examination of Self-Efficacy, Social Support, and Stress as Predictors of Psychological and Physical Distress among Hispanic College Students. *Hispanic Journal of Behavioral Sciences, 19*, 182-201.

Stephens, N. M., Fryberg, S. A., Markus, H. R., Johnson, C. S., & Covarrubias, R. (2012). Unseen disadvantage: How American universities' focus on independence undermines the academic performance of first-generation college students. *Journal of Personality and Social Psychology, 102*(6), 1178-1197. http:// dx.doi.org/10.1037/a0027143

Stephens, N. M., Hamedani, M. G., & Destin, M. (2014). Closing the Social-Class Achievement Gap: A Difference-Education Intervention Improves First-Generation Students' Academic Performance and All Students' College Transition. *Psychological Science, 25*(4), 943. http://dx.doi.org/10.1177/0956797613518349

Stolle-McAllister, K. (2011). The Case for Summer Bridge: Building Social and Cultural Capital for Talented Black STEM Students. *Science Educator, 20*(2), 12-22.

Taylor, C. M., & Howard-Hamilton, M. (1995). Student Involvement and Racial Identity Attitudes Among African American Males. *Journal of College Student Development, 36*(4), 330.

Terrion, J. L., & Leonard, D. (2010). Motivation of Paid Peer Mentors and Unpaid Peer Helpers in Higher Education. *International Journal of Evidence Based Coaching and Mentoring, 8*(1), 85-103.

Tinto, V. (1997). Colleges as Communities: Exploring the Educational Character of Student Persistence. *Journal of Higher Education, 68*, 599-623.

Walpole, M., Simmerman, H., Mack, C., Mills, J. T., Scales, M., & Albano, D. (2008). Bridge to Success: Insight into Summer Bridge Program Students' College Transition. *Journal of the First-Year Experience & Students in Transition, 20*(1), 11-30.

Woosley, S., & Shepler, D. (2011). Understanding the Early Integration Experiences of First-Generation College Students. *College Student Journal, 45*(4), 700-714.

Zimmerman, B. J. (2000). Self-Efficacy: An Essential Motive to Learn. *Contemporary Educational Psychology, 25*(1), 82-91. http://dx.doi.org/10.1006/ceps.1999.1016

Also Available from Woodhall Press

From Tom Hazuka and Dinty W. Moore, founding editor of *Brevity* literary journal, comes a new anthology that will make you *laugh out loud* in 750 words or less!

Featuring seventy-one hilarious flash essays from both established and up-and-coming writers, this anthology is perfect for students of writing and comedy—and for anybody who appreciates a good laugh!

It's funny, because it's true!

Available wherever books are sold.

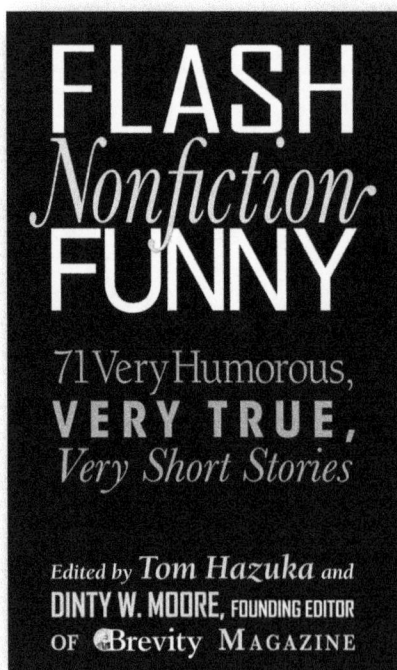

FLASH
Nonfiction
FUNNY

71 Very Humorous,
VERY TRUE,
Very Short Stories

Edited by **Tom Hazuka** and
DINTY W. MOORE, FOUNDING EDITOR
OF **Brevity** MAGAZINE

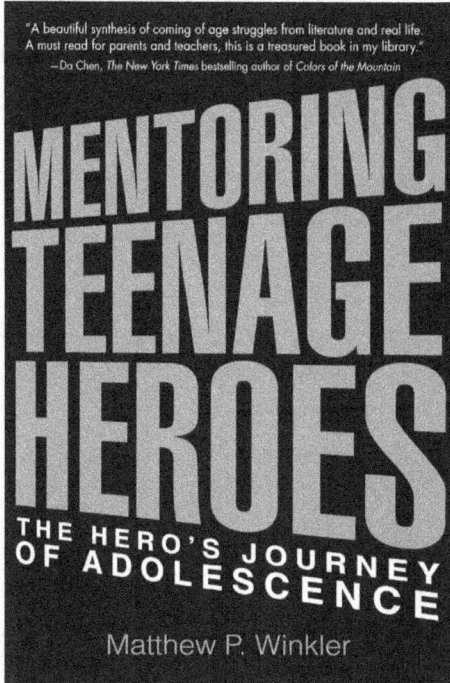

"A beautiful synthesis of coming of age struggles from literature and real life. A must read for parents and teachers, this is a treasured book in my library."
—Da Chen, *The New York Times* bestselling author of *Colors of the Mountain*

MENTORING TEENAGE HEROES

THE HERO'S JOURNEY OF ADOLESCENCE

Matthew P. Winkler

Matthew P. Winkler's viral TED-Ed lesson "What Makes a Hero?" introduced the Hero's Journey to millions of viewers. *Mentoring Teenage Heroes* is the perfect companion book, guiding parents, teachers, coaches, and other adults toward a fresh understanding of adolescence as a historic quest. For grown-ups, daily life is a routine grind. For teenagers, it's an epic struggle for identity.

Also Available from Woodhall Press

Jonathan Stein, the CEO of Apollo Aeronautics, thinks only a bad heart can stop him from reaching the moon. But when he discovers his father may have been murdered to protect an appalling NASA secret, he must decide whether his moral compass still points toward the stars. In Tom Seigel's thrilling debut, Stein must grapple with NASA's checkered past in the most personal way possible as he himself is about to lead the first mission to the moon in over thirty years. Inspired by the true story of Nazi scientists and engineers at NASA, *The Astronaut's Son* is a page-turner you won't want to miss.

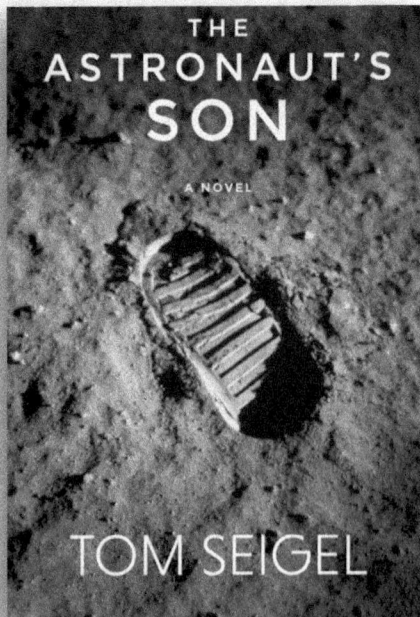

Coming Soon

woodhall press

Fall down the rabbit hole in Fall 2018 with *Alice's Adventures in #Wonderland*, Lewis Carroll's classic story retold for the digital age, and accompanied by stunning illustrations from Bats Langley.

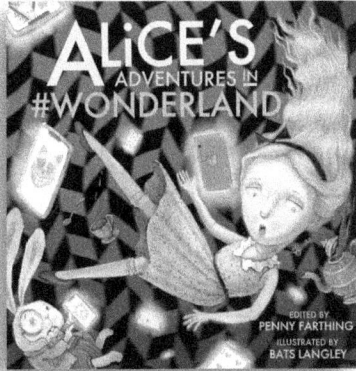

A Lion in the Snow

In this piercing essay collection, James M. Chesbro finds himself disoriented and bewildered by fatherhood again and again as he explores the maddening moments that provide occasions for new understandings about our children and us. Perfect for Father's Day, *A Lion in the Snow* is a contemporary father's field guide, a husband's compendium, and a wife's glimpse into the turning mind of a spouse in the grounded prose of domestic conflict.

Man in the (Rearview) Mirror

In an age in which everything in America is complex and complicated, *Man in the (Rearview) Mirror* explores a deeply personal and emotional journey through loss, love, and reconciliation, using the lens of a physical journey across America by a former corporate sports-writer turned Uber driver.

www.ingramcontent.com/pod-product-compliance
Lightning Source LLC
Chambersburg PA
CBHW031846090426
42741CB00005B/366